Penguin Critical Studies

The Poetry of Shelley

Michael Ferber is a Professor of English at the University of New Hampshire. He holds a Ph.D. in English from Harvard and has taught at Yale. From 1983 to 1987 he worked for nuclear disarmament at the Coalition for a New Foreign Policy in Washington. His book *The Social Vision of William Blake* was published in 1985. He is also the author of *The Poetry of William Blake* in the Penguin Critical Studies series.

Penguin Critical Studies
Advisory Editor: Bryan Loughrey

The Poetry of Shelley

Michael Ferber

Penguin Books

PENGUIN BOOKS

Published by the Penguin Group
Penguin Books Ltd, 27 Wrights Lane, London W8 5TZ, England
Penguin Books USA Inc., 375 Hudson Street, New York, New York 10014, USA
Penguin Books Australia Ltd, Ringwood, Victoria, Australia
Penguin Books Canada Ltd, 10 Alcorn Avenue, Toronto, Ontario, Canada M4V 3B2
Penguin Books (NZ) Ltd, 182–190 Wairau Road, Auckland 10, New Zealand

Penguin Books Ltd, Registered Offices: Harmondsworth, Middlesex, England

First published 1993
10 9 8 7 6 5 4 3 2 1

Typeset by Datix International Limited, Bungay, Suffolk
Set in 9/11 pt Monophoto Times
Printed in England by Clays Ltd, St Ives plc

Contents

Acknowledgements

The publishers would like to thank the following for permission to quote passages from copyright material: Cambridge University Press for 'Shelley, Dryden and Mr Eliot' in *Selected Literary Essays* by C. S. Lewis; Faber and Faber Ltd for *The Use of Poetry and the Use of Criticism* by T. S. Eliot; and Rogers, Coleridge & White Ltd for *Greek Pastoral Poetry* by Anthony Holden.

Preface

The text I quote from wherever possible is *Shelley's Poetry and Prose*, a generous selection carefully edited by Donald H. Reiman and Sharon B. Powers (New York and London: Norton, 1977).

All quotations from the Bible are in the Authorized (King James) Version. Quotations from Dante's *Divine Comedy* are in Allen Mandelbaum's translation (Berkeley: University of California Press, 1980–84). I use the following abbreviations: *PJ* is William Godwin's *Enquiry Concerning Political Justice*, third ed. (1798); *PL* is Milton's *Paradise Lost*; *PU* is Shelley's *Prometheus Unbound*. Information about Mahatma Gandhi in chapter seven is drawn from Geoffrey Ashe, *Gandhi* (New York: Stein and Day, 1968).

I would like to thank Susan Arnold, Eric Clarke, and Lauren Henry for their many suggestions for improvements, and my students Jennifer Beard, Cindi Berthelette, Todd Napolitano, and Erika Olbricht for not feeling too intimidated to make helpful comments on several chapters.

Introduction

Few poets have aroused as much controversy over as long a time as Shelley has, and probably no poet's reputation has swung to such extremes as his has, even after nearly two centuries. He is now safely ensconced in the canon of major poets taught at universities, but only after overcoming a serious challenge in the 1930s by T.S. Eliot, W.H. Auden, F.R. Leavis, and others. Whether it is due to his 'weak grasp upon the actual' (Leavis), his embarrassingly 'puerile' and 'adolescent' enthusiasms (Eliot), his elaborate poetic diction and rhetorical intricacies, or his radical views about religion and society, Shelley's poetry has not lost its power to set teeth on edge or to raise hackles. That power may be inseparable from its capacity, in many other readers from his own day to ours, to send shivers down the spine or start a fire in the brain. Some sort of energy or virtue in the poetry seems acknowledged on all sides, perhaps its tremendously inventive drive, its sometimes desperate gush of words and images, a gush none the less bound in strict poetic forms and all the more potent for that strictness. Few readers feel indifferent to it.

We shall return to his reputation at the end of this book. The book's main purpose is to help new readers of Shelley read him well. Not too much will be said to convince such readers that Shelley is a great poet, for to do that job properly would entail discussing basic political and moral issues as well as the function of literature in society, questions Shelley himself discussed at length and with great eloquence in *A Defence of Poetry*. I shall assume that readers of this book, whether out of duty or genuine interest, have agreed to take Shelley seriously and have read his major poems at least once. In the course of the discussions of individual poems I hope it will emerge without explicit argument that some of them are wonderful and others at least show Shelley's great power. Shelley is difficult at first – not as difficult as William Blake but more difficult than any of the other Romantic poets. Some of the intense reactions to Shelley, for and against, seem born of superficial acquaintance with him, or at least of a failure to grasp just how subtle his feats of style, and how thoroughly elaborated his ideas and metaphors, can be. It requires some work at first to arrive at the high pleasures of his poetry.

For that reason I have distributed rather unevenly my discussions of the poems. Some of them, such as 'Ode to the West Wind', get treated in great detail (at the rate of about a paragraph per line in this case) while others get much more summary handling or get left out altogether. I think it is more useful to the beginner to be led through a few poems slowly and closely, as examples of what Shelley does at his best, than to survey more evenly but at greater distance the full range of his work. My approach tries to do justice to Shelley's sometimes astonishing craftsmanship, which can only be fully appreciated at the level of the line, image, or word.

Percy Bysshe Shelley was born on 4 August 1792, the eldest of six children of Timothy Shelley, landowner and Whig Member of Parliament, and of Elizabeth, *née* Pilford, at Field Place, the family home, near Horsham, Sussex. He was a precocious and rather spoiled boy, quick at his early lessons in Greek and Latin, fascinated by chemistry and galvanism, indulged by his parents and the servants, and followed about by several adoring younger sisters, whom he would enlist in his scientific experiments and frighten with horrific gothic tales. His father sent him at age ten to Syon House Academy, and then two years later to Eton, where he was a brilliant pupil but a fierce nonconformist, refusing to fag (or serve as valet) to a senior pupil and bringing upon himself severe bullying by many of the boys as a result. His lifelong feeling of outrage against tyranny, stupidity, and violence must have taken root here.

At home between terms at Eton, Shelley fell in love, largely by post, with his cousin Harriet Grove, but by the end of 1810 she had put an end to their correspondence, ostensibly because of his irreligious views. 'Prejudice, Priestcraft, Opinion, and Gold' were thus added to the vices against which he vowed to fight, for, as he put it in a poem at the time, they fill the void 'Where Love ought to reign'. In the autumn of 1810 he entered University College, Oxford, where he was known as the eccentric author of two gothic novels, but in his second term he was expelled with his friend Thomas Jefferson Hogg for writing – or more precisely, for refusing to admit or deny writing – a pamphlet called *The Necessity of Atheism*. His breach with his father began here; that Sir Timothy, whose own father Bysshe was now a baronet, seemed less concerned with Shelley's beliefs than with the scandal of his expulsion only made Shelley more indignant, and hypocrisy joined his list of enemies. He soon eloped with Harriet Westbrook, a beautiful and naïve girl barely sixteen, and married her in Edinburgh, despite his convictions about free love. Sir Timothy cut off his allowance over what he considered a misalliance, though later negotiations restored some of it. Money remained a problem for the rest of Shelley's life; he was usually generous nevertheless with what he had, or expected to have; some tradesmen went for years, however, without payment. In

February 1812 he and Harriet went to Dublin, where he gave a speech and published two pamphlets on behalf of Irish independence and the best means of achieving it. In the spring they moved to Wales.

At twenty Shelley had already done and suffered too much too soon; for the next ten years he was to feel old, even 'ninety', as he wrote, and certainly older than his bland and respectable father. He was afflicted with various illnesses, real and imaginary, including possibly a venereal disease. None the less he continued to behave like a brave and brilliant revolutionary youth, with intervals of doubt and despair, until his death. He was filled to bursting with ideas and feelings that he was only slowly to bring under control; he had been writing poetry since he was ten or so, and devoured literature and philosophy in Greek, Latin, English, and French (he was later to add German, Italian, and Spanish); he carried scientific instruments with him wherever he travelled; he kept up with current political events in Britain, Ireland, the Continent, and America; and he perpetually pressed his friends, and especially young women, into his schemes for transforming the world through utopian experiments in communal living.

These same twenty years, 1792 to 1812, saw the rise and fall of the revolution in France and the upsurge and suppression of revolutionary hopes among many in Britain as well. The French Revolution reached its most radical phase in 1792 but was betrayed into the Terror by Robespierre and then confiscated by Napoleon, who went to war with all of Europe to establish a new empire. It was only in 1812 that Napoleon suffered his first irremediable defeat. In Britain the reform societies and sympathizers with the French Revolution reached their peak around 1794 but were soon suppressed by William Pitt's reactionary regime, which was at war with France from early 1793; Britain remained at war, with a brief truce, until 1815. The Whig Connection, the great landed families such as the Duke of Norfolk, Sir Timothy's patron, retreated from serious efforts at parliamentary reform, though it supported Catholic emancipation and abolition of the slave trade. The great first generation of Romantic poets, Wordsworth, Coleridge, and Southey – Shelley met Southey just before going to Ireland – at first supported reform and revolution, but by 1802 or so had abandoned it, Southey even stooping to become Poet Laureate in 1813. Meanwhile the industrial revolution, given a boost by state military spending, had already changed the relationships among all social classes.

To the personal experiences that set his character and commitments, then, we must add the continual influence, mainly discouraging, of public events. One might imagine that Shelley was destined to have been born in 1770 or 1772, like Wordsworth or Coleridge, but was held in limbo for two decades by an angel making a social experiment. Shelley had to recapitulate rapidly the spiritual history of the age by voracious reading and perhaps by re-enacting it in miniature in Field Place and Eton. Southey, in any case, saw in Shelley a younger version of himself: 'He is just what I was in 1794.' Much of the impetus of Shelley's social and political writings, which include some of his greatest poems, comes from a desire to rethink, almost to replay, the French Revolution and the upheavals in Britain, and to correct, or reject, the dereliction of the once radical poets just twenty years older than he.

It fits this impression of a time warp that Shelley should learn from Southey in 1811 that William Godwin was still alive and active in London. Godwin was the lion of intellectual radicals for a few years following the appearance of his long treatise *Political Justice* in 1793 and his novel *Caleb Williams* in 1794. Now considered a father of anarchism – 'Government,' he wrote in *Political Justice*, 'is nothing but regulated force' – he argued that only by a 'universal illumination' brought about by candid, rational conversation, and not by revolutionary violence, could humankind achieve a 'complete reformation' and a 'true euthanasia of government'. 'Benevolence' and 'public utility' are the only criteria of morality, not self-interest, and they must supersede personal gratitude to family, friends, or patrons in all our acts; we must be 'a true patriot of human kind'. These positions and several others are worked out with great clarity and without flinching from consequences that many readers felt were absurd. Many others, such as Wordsworth, were electrified by them, and revered their author. Within a year or two the public climate had turned hostile to radical philosophy, which it connected with France; many of Godwin's admirers abandoned him, and he sank into obscurity. Shelley had read some of his work and, soon after hearing about him from Southey, wrote a letter to this 'luminary too dazzling for the darkness which surrounds him', and offered him his friendship. Godwin responded, and within the year they met in London.

Godwin's other great badge of distinction or notoriety was to have been married to Mary Wollstonecraft, one of the earliest and greatest of feminists, whose book *A Vindication of the Rights of Woman* had appeared in 1792. Mary had died of complications after giving birth to their daughter, also named Mary, in 1797. In 1814, after more moving about among Wales, Ireland, and London, and after Harriet bore a daughter, Ianthe, Shelley met Mary Wollstonecraft Godwin, then sixteen, beautiful, and brilliant, and fell in love. Already convinced that his relationship with Harriet was no longer one of love, and overwhelmed by Mary's love for him, he eloped with her (and her stepsister Claire) to Switzerland. Though they returned to England after a few weeks, Shelley was never to return to

Harriet, who bore him another child, a son, late that year. When his grandfather died Shelley received funds to pay off debts and an annual allowance of £1000, of which £200 was to go to Harriet. The rest of her life was unhappy, and she ended it by suicide in late 1816. Shelley was denied custody of the children by the Court of Chancery. Meanwhile Mary had borne and lost a baby, and then had a son, William, in early 1816. Shortly after they learned of Harriet's death, the anticlerical advocate of free love and the daughter of an anarchist and a feminist got married in a church.

During a second stay in Switzerland that year Shelley had begun a friendship with Byron, only four years older than Shelley but already the most famous poet in England and perhaps the world. Claire was with them again, pursued Byron, and later bore his daughter, Allegra. Shelley meanwhile had begun writing the poems for which he is remembered, *Queen Mab* (while still with Harriet), *Alastor*, 'Hymn to Intellectual Beauty', and 'Mont Blanc'; in 1817 he wrote his longest poem, *Laon and Cythna*, an epic of revolution and love. Mary, it turned out, could also write, and after several days of conversations with Shelley, Byron, and Polidori about how to write ghost stories she set about producing *Frankenstein*; it was published in late 1817 (dated 1818) to sensational reviews, and within five years was performed on stage. She continued to write novels, stories, and essays long after Shelley's death.

Two other friends deserve mention. Thomas Love Peacock was a poet seven years Shelley's senior; his enthusiasm for the Greeks was contagious, and he later wrote a witty send-up of the Shelley household in one of his 'crotchet' novels called *Nightmare Abbey* (1818). (The caricature of Shelley called Scythrop was well received by the original, despite its misrepresentation of his views. See Appendix.) Leigh Hunt was a year older than Peacock and like him could serve as mentor to the younger poet. He too was a poet and a political radical, but he is best remembered as an editor and warm encourager of such new talents as Byron and Keats as well as Shelley. He and his brother served a two-year stint in prison for libelling the Prince Regent in their journal the *Examiner* in 1813.

In March 1818 Shelley, Mary, their two children (Clara was born in 1817), Claire, Claire's daughter, and two servants left England for Italy. Shelley was never to return from this 'paradise of exiles' and nearly all of his greatest poetry was written in Rome, Naples, Pisa, Lucca, or Florence. Not that he was happy. Clara died in 1818, and the beloved three-year-old William died the next year. A time of alienation from Mary seemed to follow on these deaths, and there were additional burdens concerning children: Allegra, whom Byron insisted on keeping from Claire, and a possible illegitimate child of Shelley's. His health, too, was precarious and rather mysterious, and it did not help his health or his relations with Mary that for a time he was in love with Claire. He kept up an extensive correspondence with friends and publishers in England and followed political events there, such as the Peterloo Massacre of 1819, which prompted him to write *The Mask of Anarchy*, his best political broadside. He completed *Prometheus Unbound* in 1819, as well as *The Cenci* and 'Ode to the West Wind'. Another son, Percy Florence, was born in that year, the only child of Mary's to survive childhood.

The household moved frequently throughout Italy, and Shelley made additional trips alone to see Byron, but despite these constant disruptions and despite poor sales and poorer reviews in England he continued to produce poetry, essays, and translations at an impressive rate. An infatuation with an unavailable young aristocratic woman, Teresa Viviani, led to *Epipsychidion* in early 1821. When the young poet Keats died of tuberculosis in Rome that year, Shelley honoured him with a pastoral elegy, *Adonais*, perhaps his most carefully wrought poem. Shelley always loved to sail, and in 1822 he received a boat made to his order and named the *Don Juan* after Byron's greatest poem and hero. Caught in a storm off the coast near Leghorn the boat capsized and Shelley and his friend Edward Williams were drowned. Shelley was twenty-nine. His body was washed ashore and cremated by Byron, Hunt, and Edward Trelawny, and later the ashes were buried in the Protestant Cemetery of Rome, where Keats lay. Mary remained in Italy another year, and then returned to England, where she edited Shelley's works and wrote her own until her death in 1851.

Told as briefly as this, Shelley's life sounds frantic and unaccountable, if not insane. Certainly he was often seized with vehement and even violent impulses, but he yielded to those impulses not only out of self-indulgence or youthful folly. He had deep convictions about the sacredness of love, of forthright sincerity, and of the duty to resist tyranny and superstition wherever they are met. His generosity led him to improvident squandering. His indignation drew him into fights he could not win. Sometimes his damn-the-consequences bravado, such as signing a guestbook 'atheist' in a Swiss inn he knew was frequented by Britons, led to unnecessary but inevitable scandal. To disapprove of him as an 'adolescent', however, as T.S. Eliot did, is tacitly to approve as 'mature' a set of compromises with the violent, reactionary, tradition-bound, corrupt, and hypocritical society and government of Regency England, and Shelley could seldom bring himself to make such compromises. However his beliefs arose, and whatever his personal faults, to dismiss Shelley is to come dangerously close to dismissing human hope, which Shelley made one of his great themes. It is to reject the 'beautiful idealisms of moral excellence' that might inspire us to reform a society that always needs it. It is to turn one's back on youth and the possibility of rejuvenating this wintry world. It must feel like death to have a heart so narrow as to have no room in it for Shelley's poetry.

1   *Queen Mab*

Shelley was so intensely aware of the many evils of English and Irish society – governmental tyranny, religious bigotry, mass slaughter on battle-fields, great disparities of wealth, selfish commercial practice, rigid marriage laws, disease, and poor diet, to name the chief ones – and he held so many deep convictions about what the ideal society should be like and how we might bring it about, that much of his short life was given to a restless search for the best way to reach the public with his message. He tried pamphlets, public speeches, handbills, and letters; he dropped leaflets from balconies and slipped them into the pockets of passers-by; he even launched propaganda in bottles and little hot-air balloons (and wrote a sonnet about each of these vehicles). Though he wrote poems constantly, sometimes on public themes, he seemed at first to consider prose as better suited to his aims. He had little luck with it, however. A pamphlet on atheism led to his dismissal from Oxford, his servant spent six months in jail for posting handbills, and most of the nautical and aerial missives ended up in the files of the Home Office, which kept an eye on this troublesome young radical. He was better received in Ireland, but suppression of dissent in England was too thorough and severe for him to hope for normal publication.

In 1812, while living in Wales, Shelley conceived another ploy and began his first major poem, *Queen Mab*. Running to some 2,300 lines in nine cantos, not counting the notes, it tells of a young woman's dream in which Queen Mab shows her all the evils Shelley hated and all the blessings of the society he hoped for. When he had written a little of it he wrote to a publisher, Thomas Hookham, that despite its radical teachings 'a Poem is safe, the iron-souled Attorney General would scarcely dare to attack "Genus irritabile vatum"' ('the sensitive race of poets', from Horace). To think that versifying his opinions would protect him from prosecution was naïve, and in the end he settled on a small private printing. He had other censors to outwit first, however, such as the sort of parents who suppressed his affair with Harriet Grove, so he asked that the poem be printed in a 'small neat Quarto, on fine paper & so as to catch the aristocrats: They will not read it, but their sons and daughters may.' This equivalent of a plain brown envelope no doubt included the title, which affords no clue that the long lectures the title character gives to an innocent young woman are deeply subversive. If the aristocrats remembered their Shakespeare they would recognize Queen Mab from Mercutio's speech in *Romeo and Juliet* (I.4.53–103): she is 'the fairies' midwife' who drives her tiny chariot over sleepers at night, making lovers dream of love, courtiers of curtsies, lawyers of fees, parsons of benefices, and soldiers of 'cutting foreign throats'. It sounds harmless enough, perhaps, though a glance at anything after canto II would have made it obvious that this midwife of dreams is the opposite of Mercutio's, for she raises the dreamer out of selfish interests into a vast disinterested view of the world, still the object of desire, to be sure, but the highest object of a selfless desire. (Shelley was to rewrite Mercutio's speech a second time in 'The Witch of Atlas' [1820], whose title character makes people dream of their opposite, and better, selves.) And this olympian disinterest very much conflicted with the interests of the aristocrats.

The Queen Mab framework was probably also designed to get the sons and daughters to open the book once it got past their fathers and mothers, and the verse, a mixture of blank verse and shorter unrhymed lyrical forms inspired by Southey's popular romances, was designed to keep them reading. The title and the pretty poetry are the honey that rims the cup of bitter medicine, as the Roman poet Lucretius puts it in a simile for the verse of his own long philosophical poem, *On the Nature of Things* (*De Rerum Natura*), a poem Shelley had loved since studying it at Eton (he quotes it once in the epigraph and twice in the notes). Today it is harder for us to appreciate the sweet taste of mere verse, and if we read philosophy we prefer it neat. For his day Shelley was not naïve to think that passably good verse would delight as well as teach, as Horace said, and his verse in many stretches is more than passably good.

Ianthe is asleep as the poem opens, in a 'baby Sleep' (I.40), while Henry, unnamed until the final canto (IX.183), hovers solicitously over her bed. She has not been well, apparently, and he is uncertain at first if death or sleep prevails. Queen Mab descends in her chariot, the first of many chariots that run or fly through Shelley's poetry, and stands by the girl she has singled out for instruction. 'Soul of Ianthe! thou, / Judged alone worthy of the envied boon, / That waits the good and the sincere' (I.122–4). Ianthe's soul is told to 'Awake! Arise!' (I.129), and as it does so, 'Each stain of earthliness / Had passed away, it reassumed / Its native dignity, and stood / Immortal amid ruin' (I.135–8). This transformation, so like the Christian belief in the resurrection, not only reflects the Platonic dualism that Shelley entertained alongside the Lucretian materialism but also prepares us for the utter transformation of the earth and human society that the Fairy reveals in the last two cantos, where 'All things are recreated' (VIII.107). It may also be Shelley's answer to the problem posed implicitly by Godwin's standard of universal benevolence, namely, how do we achieve it? How do we transcend self-interest or self-love? How, to put it in more modern terms, can we acquire an objective view of the totality beyond the subjective distortions of ideology? Or, to borrow the terms of the epigraph from Archimedes that precedes the poem, where is the standpoint from which to move the world? Mab is Shelley's answer. We dream this transcendent perspective in our souls, while our bodies, those sites of selfish cares, lie asleep.

That is not as foolish as it sounds to the worldly wise, but a defence of Shelley on dreams would draw us far ahead of this poem. He had, in any case, a long literary tradition behind him. Ianthe and the Fairy ascend in the 'car of magic' (I.201) far above the earth, from which the ocean looks 'Calm as a slumbering babe', much as Ianthe herself looks while still asleep below (I.223), and still farther, until they arrive at the Temple of the Spirit of Nature and the Hall of Spells out among the heavenly spheres. In this dream-voyage Shelley had precedents at least as old as Cicero and as recent as Volney, the French revolutionary writer he much admired, and his friend Peacock; the latter two both wrote of a dream-vision prompted by the ruins of Palmyra, which is the first sight Shelley's Fairy points out in canto II.

Of the fabulous ruins of Palmyra, reports of which had entranced the British public since the 1750s, 'What now remains?' the Fairy asks. Only 'the memory / Of senselessness and shame' (II.113–14). The same is true of the pyramids and 'old Salem's haughty fane' (II.137), the Temple that Solomon built the same way the pharaohs built the pyramids, through slave labour. 'Oh! many a widow, many an orphan cursed / The building of that fane' (II.141–2). In the Temple 'an inhuman and uncultured race / Howled hideous praises to their Demon-God' (II.149–50). We may admire the way Shelley slides from the arrogant tyranny of Rome and Egypt, both safe topics, to the same trait in Solomon, a little closer to home though well attested in the Bible, and then to that of the Hebrew God, who is officially the same God Christians worship. As for Christians, there is Rome, another ruin: 'Where Cicero and Antoninus lived, / A cowled and hypocritical monk / Prays, curses and deceives' (II.179–81). All this might nevertheless pass a liberal-minded English father, browsing in a bookshop for something to give his daughter; it is all right to criticize the Jews and the Catholics; every monk is hypocritical, after all, in those gothic novels that were still popular. Moreover, this is all in the past, as the Fairy says.

With canto III, however, the Fairy unveils the present, and we see that nothing much has changed. 'Behold a gorgeous palace' where dwells 'The

King, the wearer of a gilded chain / That binds his soul to abjectness, the fool / Whom courtiers nickname monarch, whilst a slave / Even to the basest appetites' (III.22, 30–33). Drawing from Volney, Godwin, and Tom Paine, among others, Shelley's Fairy presents an impressive jeremiad against monarchy. The point that kings and slaves are really alike in their abjectness, which he repeats in the next canto – 'Aye, art thou not the veriest slave that e'er / Crawled on the loathing earth?' (IV.246–7) – becomes a distinctively Shelleyan position throughout his works. It is monarchy itself, or Power itself, that infects everyone in a society ruled by it. In France a Robespierre replaced a Louis, and a Bonaparte replaced a Robespierre, just as in England a Cromwell replaced a Charles, and another Charles replaced a Cromwell, because in neither country was the principle of monarchy extirpated. Blake made a similar point when he changed a line in his great poem, 'London' (1792), from 'german forged links' to 'mind-forg'd manacles': it is not the particular Hanoverian tyrant that enslaves us, but the habit of tyranny in our minds. As the Fairy says,

> The man
> Of virtuous soul commands not, nor obeys.
> Power, like a desolating pestilence,
> Pollutes whate'er it touches; and obedience,
> Bane of all genius, virtue, freedom, truth,
> Makes slaves of men, and, of the human frame,
> A mechanized automaton.
>
> (III.174–80)

How shall we get rid of kings and kingship? By gradual enlightenment, as Godwin said, the 'true euthanasia of government' (*PJ* 248). 'Enlightenment,' Kant wrote in 1794, 'is man's emergence from his self-imposed immaturity.' In a similar metaphor Godwin wrote that adherents of the existing social order believe that man must remain in 'perpetual pupillage' (*PJ* 296). Paine, too, mocked the childishness of kingly titles and perquisites. But Shelley visualizes it wonderfully. The day will come

> When man's maturer nature shall disdain
> The playthings of its childhood; – kingly glare
> Will lose its power to dazzle; its authority
> Will silently pass by; the gorgeous throne
> Shall stand unnoticed in the regal hall,
> Fast falling to decay

– like the ruins of Palmyra and Jerusalem (III.131–6). As we read this we may remember that Ianthe is Queen Mab's pupil right now, but she will attain her maturity at the end of her lessons. She is both a symbol of the British people whose education Shelley sought, and a future instrument of that education, a joint-labourer with Henry-Shelley.

The Fairy Queen, however, is not a modern teacher in the manner of Rousseau or Mary Wollstonecraft, who encouraged questioning and experimentation from pupils. She only lectures and unveils her audio-visual aids, while Ianthe mainly looks and listens. Since Ianthe is also a stand-in for the daughters and sons Shelley hoped to reach, we must conclude that Shelley had not given much thought either to education or to the pedagogic potential of dramatic or dialogic form. 'My opinion,' he wrote in 1811, 'is that all poetical beauty ought to be subordinate to the inculcated moral.' His opinion was to change, but one gets the impression that 'my opinion' was always the most important thing, whatever it was, and inculcation of it, somehow or other, the next most important thing. Still, it *was* his opinion that thought should be set free and that no one should fear to follow strange ideas, wherever they may lead. He had simply failed to think through the implications of that opinion for pedagogy or poetry.

And so the Fairy lectures on, like a professor at Eton or Oxford, but it is an impressive performance. She begins canto IV with a lurid scene of slaughter in battle (Napoleon's disastrous invasion of Russia had recently been in the newspapers), and draws the moral that 'From kings, and priests, and statesmen, war arose', and not from man's putatively evil nature (IV.76–80). 'War is the statesman's game, the priest's delight, / The lawyer's jest, the hired assassin's trade', and the very bread that 'royal murderers' eat (IV.168–72). She also announces her monist metaphysics: 'Soul is the only element' (IV.140). This may be the right thing to say to Ianthe's soul, but we may wonder about her body still lying asleep down below. The Fairy does not solve this problem, for her main object is the Lucretian one of refuting the religious superstitions of the age, especially 'God, Hell, and Heaven', foisted on us by hypocritical clerics (IV.210). Unlike the materialist Lucretius she argues that 'Every grain / Is sentient both in unity and part, / And the minutest atom comprehends / A world of loves and hatreds' (IV.143–6), but like Lucretius she can use her theory of cosmic self-sufficiency against the dogmas of creation, incarnation, resurrection, and the like. Shelley wrote to Southey in early 1812, 'I believe that God is another signification for the Universe.' Spinoza was expelled from his synagogue as an atheist for saying that, as Shelley knew, but it is a particular sort of atheism that allows Shelley, or his Fairy Queen, to address the 'Spirit of Nature' or 'Nature's soul' (III.226, IV.89) as the true counterpart of the vengeful tyrant who stands outside the universe and whom the church or synagogue requires us to worship as God.

Canto V is a diatribe against commerce and its origin in what the Fairy calls 'suicidal selfishness' (V.16). One could long ponder the paradoxes implicit in that brilliant phrase, but the main point is that selfishness succeeds only in the short run; in the long run it blights the heart and then decays and dies. Selfishness is the 'Twin-sister of religion' (V.22) because religion – always a pejorative term in Shelley – bribes its believers with the rewards of heaven or frightens them with threats of hell. Shelley, it must be said, bribes believers in his own system with the 'delight' and 'love' that will spring from it (V.19), but for him they are the natural and this-worldly consequences of a life well lived.

Commerce blights the world. Like monarchy, which turns both sovereign and subject into slaves, commerce ruins rich and poor alike.

> Commerce! beneath whose poison-breathing shade
> No solitary virtue dares to spring,
> But poverty and wealth with equal hand
> Scatter their withering curses, and unfold
> The doors of premature and violent death [.]

> (V.44 8)

Luxury destroys the health as well as the hearts of the rich, while it grinds the majority into the dust of misery. The industrial revolution was now far enough along for horrific descriptions of it to have found literary expression. Moralists and poets had been particularly interested in the stultifying effects of the division of labour. 'The man whose whole life is spent in performing a few simple operations,' Adam Smith wrote in *The Wealth of Nations* (1776), 'of which the effects too are, perhaps, always the same, or very nearly the same . . . generally becomes as stupid and ignorant as it is possible for a human creature to become.' Schiller in *The Aesthetic Education of Man* and Hölderlin in *Hyperion* introduced the idea into German thought. Blake wrote of the labourer forced 'In ignorance to view a small portion & think that All' (*Jerusalem* 65.27), and Godwin in his novel *Fleetwood* reported the 'stupid and hopeless vacancy' on the faces of child operatives. Beside these Shelley's passage deserves to take its place:

> . . . slaves by force or famine driven,
> Beneath a vulgar master, to perform
> A task of cold and brutal drudgery;
> Hardened to hope, insensible to fear,
> Scarce living pulleys of a dead machine,
> Mere wheels of work and articles of trade,
> That grace the proud and noisy pomp of wealth!

> (V.72 8)

But commodification has permeated society beyond the mines and factories. 'All things are sold', the Fairy says; 'the very light of heaven / Is venal' (V.177–8), alluding probably to Pitt's high tax on windows but perhaps also suggesting the venality of churchmen with their tithes. 'Even love is sold' (V.189), and a long note explains how 'Prostitution is the legitimate offspring of marriage and its accompanying errors', errors such as making one's wife into one's property, and compelling couples who despise each other to remain bound together. Buying and selling, 'the blighting bane / Of commerce' (V.193–4), is at the root of all this. But 'There is a nobler glory', which is 'The consciousness of good, which neither gold, / Nor sordid fame, nor hope of heavenly bliss / Can purchase' (V.214, 223–5). The reward of virtue is consciousness of it. Yet just as there is a kind of non-God higher than the Christian God, there is a wealth higher than gold, 'Reason's rich stores', and a higher commerce, a 'commerce of sincerest virtue', where those stores are exchangeable for 'human weal' (V.230–36).

Ianthe's spirit finally speaks at the opening of canto VI, but only to ask if there is no hope in store. There is. A few who are endowed with reason and virtue will arise to defeat falsehood and 'soon' nature will erase 'the blood-stained charter of all woe', religion (VI.55). The rest of the canto is a history of religion, and especially Christianity with its insufferable God, both of which are now in their senility. The higher counterpart of religion and God, as we saw, is the Spirit of Nature, and her other name, we now learn, is Necessity. Every atom of the universe plays a predestined part guided by this Spirit. 'Spirit of Nature! all-sufficing Power, / Necessity! thou mother of the world! / Unlike the God of human error, thou / Requirest no prayers or praises' (VI.197–200). None the less, 'A shrine is raised to thee' in 'The sensitive extension of the world. / That wondrous and eternal fane, / Where pain and pleasure, good and evil join, / To do the will of strong necessity' (VI.226, 231–4). This is probably the first and last time a beautiful young woman has been called a sensitive extension of the world in a poem, but Shelley's logical consistency deserves admiration. The image is in any case a variant of the Christian idea of the body as a temple of the soul: here both body and soul are a temple of Necessity.

Except as a way of preserving the rhetorical power of prayer or praise while rejecting any God that can be praised or prayed to, however, it is difficult to see why Shelley wants to personify Necessity and address her in such excited tones. Lucretius also wanted to remove the gods from any possible intercession in human or natural events, and like Shelley he invokes a goddess (Venus) whose power permeates all things. Like Shelley too, Lucretius encountered grave difficulties with the question of necessity and free will. Shelley draws concepts from Plato and the French materialists as well as Lucretius, and especially from Godwin, who was a thorough-going environmentalist (in the psychological sense), that is, one who holds that human beings are creatures of their circumstances or education. The moral qualities of man are due entirely to the 'empire of impression', Godwin wrote, and if you knew all the circumstances of an action you could predict it, for 'all actions are necessary' – they are the result of the strongest motives (*PJ* 107, 336). That this theory made man passive, as Godwin conceded, would seem to be its fatal defect if one retained any hope of rousing one's fellow creatures to reform their society. Karl Marx wrestled with the same dilemma (it is interesting that he wrote his doctoral dissertation on the problem of free will in Epicurus and Lucretius), and fundamentalist Marxists, like fundamentalist Christians, have always in-voked the inevitability of the revolution (or the revelation) while exhorting people to act on its behalf. That may be a contradiction but it seems to work: people are motivated to act when they have faith that the outcome is assured. Shelley's motive in introducing Necessity here may come from Godwin's point that the laws of necessity not only make a man act on the strongest motive but compel his understanding to assent to the strongest argument. Reason, then, is harnessed to the laws of nature as a prime mover of social revolution. 'How swift the step of reason's firmer tread,' the Fairy says (VI.59); it marches to victory to the tune of Necessity.

The next canto is a little more dramatic. Ianthe begins it by telling of a sight her mother took her to see as an infant: dark-robed priests burning an unrepentant atheist at the stake. 'I wept. / "Weep not, child!" cried my mother, "for that man / Has said, 'There is no God'"' (VII.11–13). (This unspeakable mother may be Shelley's caricature of Harriet Grove's mother; we may also wonder just where in Britain in the 1790s Ianthe's mother might have found an execution of a heretic by burning.) Queen Mab responds, 'There is no God! / Nature confirms the faith his death-groan sealed' (VII.13–14), and launches another vigorous attack on religion. She shortly brings in a guest lecturer, however, who is a peculiar authority on the evils of Christianity, Ahasuerus the legendary Wandering Jew. His lecture is also dramatic, for it encloses a dialogue between Moses and God as well as his own brief exchange with Christ. Shelley was fascinated with this legend, which tells of a Jew who mocked Christ on the way to Calvary and was punished for his mockery, as if in parody of the eternal life Christ promised his followers, with endless life on earth. Shelley's earliest long poem, composed in 1809 and 1810, was called 'The Wandering Jew: or the

Victim of the Eternal Avenger'; the subtitle indicates where the author's sympathy lay. The Jew shows up again in one of Shelley's two gothic novels, *St Irvyne*, written at about the same time, and he will reappear in his last drama, *Hellas* (1821).

Seeking a second opinion, Ianthe asks Ahasuerus, 'Is there a God?' and he replies: 'Is there a God! – aye, an almighty God, / And vengeful as almighty!' (VII.83–5). He tells the whole horrible story: how a 'murderer' (VII.100) from Egypt (Moses) was commanded by the voice of Jehovah to lead his people until they 'Wade on the promised soil through woman's blood' (VII.119); how Jehovah will torture forever every soul who lives on earth before the Redeemer comes (because they do not believe in him in advance) and most souls who live afterwards; how virtue, pure thoughts, and genius will not suffice to save us but only Jehovah's arbitrary 'grace' (VII.140). With the Incarnation, with Jehovah 'Veiling his horrible Godhead in the shape / Of man', Christ came to teach 'justice, truth, and peace, / In semblance' (not the real things) as well as zeal and the duty of propagating the faith by the sword (VII.164–72). Knowing what slaughter lay in store, Ahasuerus on Good Friday cried, '"Go! go!" in mockery' (VII.179). In the long centuries since then, Ahasuerus has seen little but bloodshed and blind revenge in the name of this God, while he himself remains steadfast in his 'defiance' of this God's curse, wandering the world but inwardly 'peaceful, and serene, and self-enshrined' (VII.256), and even optimistic that reason is even now 'Establishing the imperishable throne / Of truth' (VII.246–7).

Since the Fairy has said there is no God, and Ahasuerus says there is one, we are alerted that the Jew's speech may not be the final truth, but only the truth 'in semblance'. He seems to believe in the existence of this God, but he stresses that we hear his voice through the mediation of Moses (VII.101), as if the whole thing is a delusion or an imposture by the author of the Pentateuch. The Incarnation, however, he describes as if it really happened, and he nowhere grasps the human reality of Jesus. In his note Shelley distinguishes between 'the pretended character of this being as the Son of God and the Saviour of the world, and his real character as a man, who, for a vain attempt to reform the world, paid the forfeit of his life to that overbearing tyranny which has since so long desolated the universe in his name.' Though Ahasuerus, as an enemy of God, sees things with sharp moral clarity, he is still in the grip of an illusion. On the other hand, he sees the day of reason coming, which will release him from God's vengeance and let him die. Like Shelley's later hero Prometheus, then, he seems to stand for the history of revolutionary thought, always the highest thought of humanity at any time, but only now extricating itself from its

17

last errors and arriving at the fullness of truth. That truth includes the nonexistence of God in the first place and hence the needlessness of continual defiance. When we arrive at it, Ahasuerus' view of things will evaporate. As if to enact his imminent departure from the world, at the Fairy's command he flees as 'shapes of mingled shade and mist' (superstitions) 'Flee from the morning beam' (of enlightenment) (VII.269–71). Ahasuerus and his story make a wonderfully complex parable. In the last lines of the canto Ahasuerus is described as 'this phantasmal portraiture / Of wandering human thought' (VII.274–5). He is phantasmal not only because he is in Ianthe's dream but also because within her dream he is the memory of the present, soon to become the past, and because it is wandering or erroneous human thought that has portrayed him. 'Of', however, is ambiguous: wandering human thought is also portrayed truthfully in him. It is thought capable of seeing evil clearly and defying evil's threats as it wanders through the dark centuries towards the inevitable dawn.

After this climax, the moment has come to show Ianthe the future. The veil of time is rent, and she sees, or rather she hears, the renovated earth:

> Earth was no longer hell;
> Love, freedom, health had given
> Their ripeness to the manhood of its prime,
> And all its pulses beat
> Symphonious to the planetary spheres:
> Then dulcet music swelled
> Concordant with the life-strings of the soul;
> It throbbed in sweet and languid beatings there,
> Catching new life from transitory death [.]
>
> (VIII.14–22)

This is the first of many lyrical passages in Shelley's work concerning music. Music always pervades his descriptions of the ideal future society, or premonitions of it; indeed music *is* a premonition of it, perhaps even more than poetry. Shelley is drawing, of course, from the ancient tradition of the music of the spheres (Ianthe is, after all, up there among the spheres in her dream), audible to pure spirits after death or, more rarely, to living souls that achieve enlightenment. Shelley also seems to have thought of music as the quintessentially utopian art, just as he imagines his utopias in musical terms. Perhaps because music is pure form, while at the same time seeming to strike emotional chords (or cords) deep within us, it inspires feelings both serene and profound and it embraces something both inner and outer – like an ideal society where we feel no boundary between ourselves and others. Nietzsche was to speculate that music belongs to a culture where the dominion of violent men has already come to an end. The final act of *Prometheus Unbound*, Shelley's most sustained expression of his utopian vision, is wholly devoted to the singing and dancing of the universe. The music Ianthe hears also enacts the renewal of life from death, making death seem as transitory as the dying falls or cadences of a symphony or choral song, where one voice or instrument catches the melody completed by another and gives it new life. A catch is a musical form itself, and Shelley's use of 'catching' here summons up the ghost of the phrase 'catch one's death'. It may also remind us of Henry at his watch by Ianthe's bed below, 'Whose sleepless spirit waits to catch / Light, life and rapture from her smile' (I.29–30, repeated at IX.210–11).

Music is also the medium of love. Joy comes to Ianthe's spirit, 'Such joy as when a lover sees / The chosen of his soul in happiness, / . . . Sees her unfaded cheek / Glow mantling in first luxury of health' (VIII.32–3, 36–7). We think of Henry again, but though we have no grounds to question the selflessness of his love we may take Ianthe's love for the new world as a higher thing, at least as a more universal love or sympathy. It is one of Shelley's prime missions throughout his works to direct our capacity for passionate love, or *eros*, towards a society, towards a world. It is a disconcerting goal, easily written off as the product of the escapist day-dreams of a lovelorn adolescent, but it also gives blood to the anaemic notions of 'brotherly love' or 'universal benevolence', so easily acknowledged by tepid liberals. William Morris was to imagine his future utopia as coming about because 'the great motive power of the change was a longing for freedom and equality, akin if you please to the unreasonable passion of the lover' (*News from Nowhere* [1890], chap. 17), and more than one of the great reformers and revolutionaries of our time has confessed to such a passion, to such a love.

As Queen Mab reveals it, the idyllic new world is not just an idyllic human world, but a peaceable kingdom where tigers no longer eat lambs and the tilt of the earth's axis has been corrected to make a perpetual spring. 'All things are recreated, and the flame / Of consentaneous love inspires all life' (VIII.107–8). Not only tigers but humans have forsworn flesh; birds and beasts no longer flee from humans but gather round; 'All things are void of terror: man has lost / His terrible prerogative, and stands / An equal amidst equals' (VIII.225–7). A long note is attached here on the vegetarian diet, which Shelley adopted in 1812 and stayed with more or less consistently for the rest of his life. He believed that meat-eating was responsible for most if not all human disease, and that if we gave it up (along with alcohol) we would live long and healthy lives. His

19

note includes a charmingly bizarre interpretation of the Prometheus story (taken from a vegetarian tract by J.F. Newton), of interest because of the much profounder version Shelley will create in a few years; on this reading Prometheus' theft of fire meant the beginning of meat-eating (for there was no need to cook vegetables), and the vulture that ate his liver meant disease preying on man's vitals (it is also poetic justice). In a possible allusion to Pandora's box, part of the same myth, Shelley adds, 'All vice arose from the ruin of healthful innocence.'

As canto IX continues the picture of the future, we learn that reason and passion will work harmoniously, rather as Adam and Eve did before the fall (according to Milton): passion will go wild through the woods gathering strange flowers but will always return to her sober sister, reason, to bind a garland on her brow (IX.50–56). Death comes gently after a full life, 'almost without a fear' (IX.59). Palaces now are heaps of ruins, winds sing a dirge in roofless cathedrals, children play in mouldering prison-courts. 'Thus human beings were perfected, and earth, / Even as a child beneath its mother's love, / Was strengthened in all excellence, and grew / Fairer and nobler with each passing year' (IX.134–7).

With that the Fairy ends her lecture: 'My task is done: / Thy lore is learned' (IX.140–41). She then appeals to Ianthe's spirit to 'bravely hold thy course' and 'fearlessly bear on' through all adversity till the promised spring (IX.146, 164–70), and exhorts her to fear not death, which is but the voyage of an hour, and to keep her hopes alive, which the scene conjured by the fairy has confirmed. The spirit is sent down to be reunited with her sleeping body, and she awakes to behold Henry kneeling by her couch.

The emphasis on death is puzzling. The startling opening lines (after the dedication to Harriet) in retrospect seem irrelevant to the main theme:

> How wonderful is Death,
> Death and his brother Sleep!
> One, pale as yonder waning moon
> With lips of lurid blue;
> The other, rosy as the morn
> When throned on ocean's wave
> It blushes o'er the world:
> Yet both so passing wonderful!
>
> (I.1–8)

Perhaps they are both wonderful because in both states we travel to the land of our desire; at least we do so in sleep, while death, we are to believe, is sleep's brother. Shelley always clung to the hope of an afterlife or immortality, though not with our present consciousness of self. The Fairy claims that 'Death is a gate of dreariness and gloom, / That leads to azure isles and beaming skies / And happy regions of eternal hope' (IX.161–3). It is nevertheless hard to resist the hunch that Shelley had been looking for an impressive opening to his poem no matter how tangential to its subject; it is almost as if he anticipated Edgar Allen Poe's claim that the most poetical of all subjects is the death of a beautiful woman. Shelley's first readers could not have known that Harriet had often spoken of suicide, and that, even while expecting her first child (to be named Ianthe), she sometimes felt hopeless. When the Fairy asks Ianthe's spirit if she was not stung by hope 'When to the moonlight walk by Henry led, / Sweetly and sadly thou didst talk of death?' (IX.183–4), the Fairy seems to be alluding to private events in the lives of Harriet and Percy Shelley, and it is reasonable for the rest of us to find that exclusive reference a blemish on the poem.

If Shelley has failed to include within his poem all the evidence we need to interpret it, his sense of craft, and no doubt his fascination with the subject of death itself, led him to circle back to it in the end. The framework adds a further element of the unreal, the transcendent, to the Fairy's revelation, but perhaps it also encases the revelation in a despair-proof container, like the shell around a pearl. Perhaps Shelley was trying to say, yes, I know the world is a charnel-house and there is no visible reason to go on living in it, but there is an invisible reason, which may come to us in dreams, the substance of things hoped for, the evidence of things not seen, which will make a present hopelessness seem as transitory as a summer cloud. If that is true, then Queen Mab has saved Ianthe's life; at the outset Ianthe was suspended doubtfully between sleep and death, while at the end her soul awakens.

Queen Mab was published in 1813 in a limited edition of only 250 copies, some seventy of which were distributed by the time Shelley died. Pirated editions appeared in 1821 in both London and America, and it began to sell. Shelley was not gracious about this late success, and asked his agent to publish his disapproval; 'inasmuch as I recollect,' he added, 'it is villainous trash; & I dare say much better fitted to injure than to serve the cause which it advocates.' He did not, it appears, reject the cause which it advocates, but he seemed more concerned that its reappearance might make it harder to get his recent work published than it already was in a climate still reactionary in politics and scandalized by his reputation. Without a disclaimer he could have been prosecuted, and as it happens the London publisher went to jail for four months. Shelley must have blushed when he remembered how Southey, who had become Poet Laureate the year *Queen Mab* first appeared, was embarrassed in 1817 by the pirating of his youthful radical play *Wat Tyler*. He mentions the Southey case in his public letter, perhaps to anticipate the inevitable comparison, perhaps to tweak the Laureate while seeking shelter under his precedent, and perhaps to arouse curiosity and increase sales while seeming to disapprove of them. One wishes he had said nothing or stood up more bravely to the Yahoos. For *Queen Mab* soon became the most popular of his works, especially among the working class, which seemed to accept the ethereal Fairy framework for the sake of the eloquent thunder within. It was published in the 1820s in large editions by the radical printer Carlisle, and it was quoted and excerpted in many Chartist journals in the 1840s. At the end of the century George Bernard Shaw called it the Chartists' Bible. If Shelley is now in heaven conducting seminars among admiring workers, one hopes he has the grace to admit that his only mistake was to aim it at the children of aristocrats. And if Mary is with him, perhaps she will admit that it was a bit condescending of her to place *Queen Mab* at the back of her collected edition (1839), under 'Juvenilia', where it has remained in most editions until recently. British workers understood it better than she.

A note about the notes. Shelley's notes are longer than the poem itself, and if they are read as they come up in the poetic text they would totally destroy its momentum and dramatic illusion. They amount to a separate treatise, or set of treatises, on several subjects, some of which in fact were later published separately. Long extracts from French, Latin, and Greek authors were included in the original languages. Three epigraphs appear after the title, one each from Voltaire, Lucretius, and Archimedes, all untranslated. It is possible that Shelley intended the epigraphs and notes as yet another disguise, as if to make the volume look like a sermon or theological tract, though this camouflage conflicts with the fairy-tale wrapping (and Voltaire's 'Ecrasez l'infâme' might give pause to an aristocratic papa). One imagines that Shelley was so filled with his cherished ideas that he had to devise a compromise between leaving many of them out for the sake of poetic art and stuffing them into a poem already dangerously didactic and long. It is probably best to read the poem first without the notes, but the notes themselves contain some of Shelley's finest prose, and they are indispensable explications of positions he never abandoned.

We may disagree with Mary Shelley's judgement that *Queen Mab* belongs with her husband's juvenile poems, but most of his readers sense that Shelley becomes Shelley – he arrives at the modes, themes, and style distinctive of his 'mature' poetry – with the poems he wrote in 1815 and early 1816 and published as *Alastor . . . and Other Poems*. This impression may owe something to the surprising contrast between the mood of the sermonizing poem of social reform of 1813 and the mood of the self-absorbed and sometimes despairing poems of two and three years later. In her note on the title poem, Mary Shelley explains that 'A very few years, with their attendant events, had checked the ardour of Shelley's hopes, though he still thought them well grounded', events not political, such as the final defeat of Napoleon and the restoration of the Bourbons in France, but personal, such as poverty, loss of friends, and the expectation that he would soon die of consumption. She considers the poem 'an outpouring of his own emotions', and if that commonplace Romantic phrase can apply to a long narrative poem then it certainly seems to fit *Alastor; or, The Spirit of Solitude*.

Recent criticism, however, has tried to demonstrate that *Alastor* is not an outpouring at all but a carefully staged dialogue of sorts between the main character and the narrator, neither of which stands for Shelley, who could not decide the issue between them. We shall look more closely at this reading, but we should note first that, whatever personal grief Shelley may have felt at the time of writing *Alastor*, within a year he was writing *Laon and Cythna*, an ambitious epic of social revolution, and within another year he was starting his optimistic masterpiece, *Prometheus Unbound*. He was to alternate between anguished personal quests and hopeful public prophecies throughout his life. We have already seen, too, that *Queen Mab* is enclosed in a meditation on death, while *Laon and Cythna*, though full of revolutionary action, is obsessed with martyrdom, so it is not always easy to separate the social poetry from the personal, nor to attribute some poems to emotional outpourings and others to calculated craft.

The first difficulty with *Alastor* is the title. A careful reader of Homer might recognize it as the name of at least three characters in the *Iliad*, but only a reader who knew Greek tragedy in the original Greek could guess at its sense as (1) a wanderer, outcast, one who is pursued by an avenging spirit, a suppliant, or (2) the avenging spirit itself. Shelley's friend Thomas Love Peacock claimed that he suggested the title to Shelley, and that an *alastor* is an evil genius, not the name of the hero. Peacock was to use the word in this sense himself in his poem *Rhododaphne* in 1818. But if we take Peacock as authoritative we not only needlessly eliminate the first sense of *alastor* (found in Aeschylus and Sophocles) but we import the tragic Greek sense of nemesis into the spirit whom the wandering poet-protagonist encounters, a spirit who is not vengeful in any moral sense and whom the poet conjures up in his own dream in the first place. The poet, moreover, pursues the spirit, not the other way round, and she is better described as a spirit of love than of solitude. On the other hand, the Preface states that 'The Poet's self-centred seclusion was avenged by the furies of an irresistible passion pursuing him to speedy ruin.' That seems to warrant Peacock's view, but many readers feel that the Preface is not consistent with the poem and should have no more weight than Peacock's comment. In any case, it is perfectly justifiable to take the title as referring to the wandering poet, either as his name or as a Greek near-synonym for 'spirit of solitude'. 'Spirit of solitude', in turn, is a good epithet for the poet, for he seems to be a spirit to those he meets, 'the Spirit of wind / With lightning eyes' (259–60), and at the end he is called a 'surpassing Spirit' (714) by the narrator himself.

Except for the opening (1–49) and closing (672–720), and one or two brief interventions, the narrator devotes the poem to the story of the life of a Poet (whom I shall capitalize henceforth, as Shelley does). 'There was a Poet,' he begins, and we never learn his name, nationality, date, or any other worldly circumstances except the route of his extraordinary journey. They are left so obviously vague that the Poet seems to be a spirit or a symbol from the first. Indeed the most important fact about him seems to be that he died young and unknown. 'There was a Poet whose untimely tomb / No human hands with pious reverence reared, / . . . – no mourning maiden decked / With weeping flowers, or votive cypress wreath, / The lone couch of his everlasting sleep' (49–57). We are immediately in the elegiac mode, in the spirit of Gray's 'Elegy Written in a Country Churchyard' and Wordsworth's 'Lines (Left upon a Seat in a Yew-tree)', both of which Shelley knew well.

The Poet's life is sketched very briefly until he sets out on his wandering quest 'To seek strange truths in undiscovered lands' (77). First he pursues 'Nature's most secret steps' (81) in volcanic caves and lonesome vales; then he visits the ruins of ancient civilizations and gazes on the mysterious hieroglyphs 'till meaning on his vacant mind / Flashed like strong inspiration, and he saw / The thrilling secrets of the birth of time' (126–8). That seems to define his quest more precisely, for he makes his way across Arabia and Persia to the vale of Kashmir which, his hieroglyphs may have told him, was the birthplace of the human race. While he had been studying these signs, however, an Arab maiden had been tending him. She was 'Enamoured, yet not daring for deep awe / To speak her love' (132–3), while for his part he seems not to have noticed her at all. When he arrives in Kashmir, in 'Its loneliest dell, where odorous plants entwine / Beneath the hollow rocks a natural bower' (146–7), he has 'a dream of hopes' (150) in which a 'veiled maid / Sate near him' (151–2) and spoke, or sang, in a voice 'like the voice of his own soul' (153). Like him she is a poet, and sings of knowledge, truth, virtue, and 'lofty hopes of divine liberty' (159), the themes of *Queen Mab* and many of Shelley's later poems. These themes lead her to sing in 'wild numbers' (163) (verses); overcome by emotion, she stops, rises, and spreads her bare arms to embrace the Poet. He rises to meet her, and she 'With frantic gesture and short breathless cry / Folded his frame in her dissolving arms' (186–7). It ends as suddenly as it began: 'Now blackness veiled his dizzy eyes, and night / Involved and swallowed up the vision; sleep, / Like a dark flood suspended in its course, / Rolled back its impulse on his vacant brain' (188–91), and he drowns, as it were, in sleep. He suddenly awakens to the cold light of morning and the 'vacant woods' (195) and 'His wan eyes / Gaze on the empty scene as vacantly / As ocean's moon looks on the moon in heaven' (200–202).

We notice that twice the Poet's mind or brain has been 'vacant' as he has gone into a visionary trance: first he learns the secrets of the hieroglyphs and then he discovers love, or an ideal beloved. They are both revelations or unveilings – indeed the maid is veiled at first, he then sees 'Her glowing limbs beneath the sinuous veil' (176), and finally she embraces him with bare arms, only to leave him veiled in blackness himself – and we seem invited to see more similarities between them. Hieroglyphs, not yet fully understood in Shelley's day, were sometimes taken to be poetry, the primordial poetry of the human race; the maiden is a poet, and one scholar has recently called her a visionary hieroglyph herself. She is, after all, only the representation of a maiden, not a real one, as hieroglyphs are representations of things, not the things themselves. Shelley was probably aware, too, of the tradition (found in Philo and others) that interpreting a sacred text is analogous to unveiling and marrying a maiden. We may wonder if the two revelations are not linked causally, for the hieroglyphs, as we noted, seem to have sent him to Kashmir, where another tradition placed the birth of the human race, if not of time itself. Perhaps there is a curse contained in the ancient writings. If his mind was vacant before the revelations, the world now seems vacant after them, and the Poet reflects that emptiness as if he has become for the moment no more than a mirror of his surroundings, a moon on the ocean reflecting the moon in the sky, itself shining with only a reflected light.

Most readers, however, have been struck with the connection between the veiled dream-maiden and the Arab maid whom the Poet neglected while pondering the hieroglyphs, and the next passage makes it explicit: 'The spirit of sweet human love has sent / A vision to the sleep of him who spurned / Her choicest gifts' (203–5). Is this spirit of love a fury or an *alastor* in Peacock's sense? Is the Poet punished for spurning love, the way Hippolytus in Euripides' play is punished for neglecting Aphrodite? The narrator may not be fair to the Poet here, for if we reread lines 129–39 we see the Poet has not so much 'spurned' the Arab maid as simply failed to notice her. We shall discuss the narrator's own biases later. It is hard to resist, meanwhile, the sense that the dream-maiden is a 'return of the repressed', as Freudians say, a version of the Arab maid herself.

In his desolation, the Poet wonders if the vision is forever lost in the 'pathless desart of dim sleep' (210) or if it may be found in sleep's paradise, through the gates of death, sleep's twin. It does not occur to him to seek her anywhere but in sleep, as if he knows that it is already too late for him to find an earthly counterpart of his ideal. The only question is whether he should seek death as a way to find her. Like the flood that rolled over his brain at the end of his dream, 'This doubt with sudden tide flowed on his heart, / The insatiate hope which it awakened, stung / His brain even like despair' (220–22). This hopeless hope, so different from the social or political hopes the maiden sang, sends him fleeing to yet remoter parts of central Asia, while death seems to have his way with him: his whitened hair sings dirges in the wind, his hand hangs like a dead bone in its withered skin – only his eyes show the fire of life. Not surprisingly, in a poem about visions, eyes are an insistent motif throughout it. As if to remind him of the Arab maiden he ignored, youthful maidens press his hand and weep as he departs from their homes.

On the 'lone Chorasmian shore' (272), probably the Caspian Sea but perhaps the Aral Sea, the Poet is struck by the contrast between a swan, now flying to its home, and his own homelessness. The words he addresses to the swan are the closest thing to a poem we actually get from this Poet, and it is a very 'poetic' utterance, for swans are ancient symbols of poets, they are said to sing when they die, and – according to Horace – they are birds of exile. All the more poignant, then, is the Poet's assumption that this swan is on his way home. At this, another 'desperate hope' leads him to contemplate suicide, though he is still doubtful if death will bring him to the realm of sleep which holds his vision. He decides to meet lone death on the sea, as if to make literal the metaphors of flooding and overwhelming we have seen, and he sets out in a little boat. In Shelley's poetry from this point on voyages in boats become as frequent as flights in chariots, and typically the voyages, like this one, are passive, the boats simply given to the winds or currents to take them where they will. This boat is blown by a whirlwind and tossed by fierce waves, but it is 'Safely fled – / As if that frail and wasted human form, / Had been an elemental god' (349–51).

At midnight on the other side of the sea the cliffs of the Caucasus appear in the moonlight, the European Caucasus if this is the Caspian, the Indian Caucasus or Hindu Kush (at a great distance) if this is the Aral. Shelley was to set *Prometheus Unbound* in the Indian Caucasus, perhaps to allude to the putative birthplace of the 'caucasian' race while shifting it eastward so as to include the oriental races, and perhaps he has the same purpose here. If so, the setting has the same significance as Kashmir earlier.

The boat is drawn into a cavern, which the Poet hails as the gate of death and the approach to his 'Vision and Love' (366), and in a mysterious movement it is taken along a river, apparently upstream (or perhaps on a tidal bore) into a whirlpool that rises in a rocky funnel until the highest ridge of water, bearing the boat, overflows the bank and deposits it safely on to a smooth spot, where a gentle breeze carries it on to a placid stream and then, presumably downstream, into a quiet cove. If, as the Poet later says to the rivulet, it is an image of his life (and rivers have been commonplace figures for human life since ancient times), then this strange voyage through the cave and upward to a stream is a journey backward through time to one's birth. We are for the third time in a setting of birth or origin.

The cove has banks 'whose yellow flowers / For ever gaze on their own drooping eyes, / Reflected in the crystal calm' (406–8). The Poet feels akin to these narcissi, and suppresses an impulse to deck his hair with them. This moment gives us a hint, if we needed one, that *Alastor* is in large part a reworking of the story of Narcissus and Echo as Ovid told it. Narcissus is a beautiful youth whom girls and boys both love, but he feels no interest in any of them. Echo, a maid who only spoke when spoken to, and whom Juno punished by limiting her speech to the last few words of another's, falls in love with Narcissus, but when she tries to embrace him he flees her touch; she wastes away and dies. Nemesis sends him to a hidden pool in the forest, and when he bends to drink he is smitten with his own image, whose eyes meet his. After many frustrating attempts to kiss his beloved, he plunges into the pool and drowns. The differences between the plots are obvious enough, but Ovid's story pervades Shelley's thoroughly enough to serve as a continuous allusion – from the 'flood' imagery and the Poet's impulse to drown himself to the Arab maid who cannot speak her love – and perhaps a framework for judging the Poet's tragic flaw.

The cove is a kind of Bower of Bliss (Spenser) or Garden of Eden, described in maternal and infantile terms. It is in a vale that the forest 'embosoms' (423). Overhead are 'meeting boughs and implicated leaves' (426), the oak 'Embraces' (433) the beech, and flowery vines or ivy

> flow around
> The grey trunks, and, as gamesome infants' eyes,
> With gentle meanings, and most innocent wiles,
> Fold their beams round the hearts of those that love,
> These twine their tendrils with the wedded boughs
> Uniting their close union [.]
>
> (440–45)

With this last simile Shelley teeters on the brink of the unbearably namby-pamby (and we may wonder how one folds a beam), but he gives us an extraordinarily vivid embodiment of nature's 'cradle'. It reminds us too of the 'cold fireside and alienated home' he left as a youth, or the 'cold home' (138) of the Arab maid: here is the regressive fantasy of what he was denied in his childhood. But nature's cradle is the Poet's 'sepulchre' (430), for he knows this is no more his home than the swan's nest had been.

Just beyond the dell is a deep well that reflects the foliage overhead and an occasional 'inconstant star' (463). The Poet looks down into it, like Narcissus, gazing into his own eyes as if it were a dream of a gloomy grave. This is the third trance the Poet falls into, and we are not surprised that 'A Spirit seemed / To stand beside him' (479–80), perhaps the one he has been pursuing all along. This time, however, she is not robed in bright light but seems identical with the woods, well, and rivulet, as if she is the *genius loci*, the spirit of that place. As he looks up, 'two eyes, / Two starry eyes, hung in the gloom of thought' (489–90) – as if he is still looking at his own two eyes in his own thought – 'And seemed with their serene and azure smiles / To beckon him' (491–2). And off he goes again.

This time he follows the rivulet downstream. As he himself proclaims, the rivulet is an image of the mystery of his life, with its darkness and brightness, unknown source and unknown course. As we can see, too, the rivulet rehearses the course of any human life, 'like childhood laughing' (499) as it begins, then flowing through 'changed' scenery, where rocks 'stemmed / The struggling brook' (527–8) and dry windlestraw grows and ancient pines 'clenched with grasping roots / The unwilling soil' (531–2). If we missed the symbolism the narrator makes it explicit in a simile:

> For, as fast years flow away,
> The smooth brow gathers, and the hair grows thin
> And white, and where irradiate dewy eyes
> Had shone, gleam stony orbs: – so from his steps
> Bright flowers departed, and the beautiful shade
> Of the green groves, with all their odorous winds
> And musical motions.
>
> (533–9)

We know that he was already old and withered by the time he came to the lone Chorasmian shore, and that he was not rejuvenated when he came to nature's cradle, so it is a little odd that his ageing and dying, however vicariously, should be repeated here. This and the other repetitions we have noted suggest that *Alastor* is only outwardly a narrative; it is really a set of variations on a theme. It is as if Shelley found the *situation* of the self-secluded and death-drawn poet so interesting in itself that he constructed a thin and artificial plot by stringing together analogous scenes.

In any case, the Poet and his river arrive at the precipice of a vast ravine. The river 'Fell into that immeasurable void / Scattering its waters to the passing winds' (569–70) but the Poet pauses, in keeping with the symbolic single rock-rooted pine that 'stretched athwart the vacancy / Its swinging boughs, to each inconstant blast / Yielding one only response' (562–4), like a wind harp, and like the Poet stretched across the vacancies of his world. And here another bower appears, the third in the poem and the fourth 'birthplace': 'a tranquil spot, that seemed to smile / Even in the lap of horror' (577–8). Ivy wraps 'entwining arms' (579) around the stones, embowering the space with leaves. There are 'children' at play here, too, this time not the ivy but bright coloured leaves, 'children of the autumnal whirlwind' (583). Flowers grow out of the blue cavern mould. Though this 'green recess' (625) is surrounded by the realm of death, it seems to signify what the Poet has always hoped, that on the far side of death's gateway there may be a paradise. The Poet does not, in any case, plunge over the cliff, but placing his hand on the old pine trunk he lays his head on an ivy-covered stone and yields to the 'final impulses' (638) of life, or death. His last sight is of the setting crescent moon. As the two tips of the horn linger at the western horizon they must look to him, as they remind us, of the eyes of the lost dream-maiden. As they sink into the dark he dies.

This long narration is enclosed, and occasionally interrupted, by more meditative and personal passages that help us characterize the Narrator. To some of his poems it may do no harm to call the narrator or *persona*, 'Shelley', but the distinction between narrator and author, possible to draw in any literary work, is often crucial in Shelley's poetry. Recent criticism of *Alastor*, as we noted at the outset, has made much of the differences between Narrator and Poet. On the model of an inconclusive prose dialogue, Shelley's *Refutation of Deism* (1814), *Alastor* can be seen as a confrontation of world views as one poet tries to understand another. The Narrator begins by invoking the 'brotherhood' (1) of the elements and cites his own 'natural piety' (3) towards 'our great Mother' (2), his love of the sequence of hours and seasons, and his kinship with bird and beast, as evidence of his fitness to tell the story of the Poet. He then invokes the 'Mother of this unfathomable world' (18) and tells how he has 'loved / Thee ever, and thee only' (19–20), pursuing her mysteries day and night, and though failing to penetrate her 'inmost sanctuary' (38) he is ready for her inspiring breath 'as a long-forgotten lyre' (42) receives the wind. These and other details of the opening section seem to define the Narrator as a nature-poet, bound by the natural world and more or less content to be so bound, much like the author of *Queen Mab*. The Poet, on the other hand, has rightly or wrongly gone beyond nature, seeking union with a transcendent spirit or ideal self, denying natural human ties, and hovering on the brink of the supernatural world. The mutual love between the Narrator and nature is embodied in the bowers the Poet visits, but these, as we saw, do not satisfy the Poet or restore him to health.

But lest we think the Narrator's natural limits must serve as the frame of reference for judging the Poet, we find, besides the sympathy and admiration shown for the Poet during his wanderings, the Narrator's expression of irretrievable loss in the final section. There the Narrator wishes he had the power of a witch or alchemist, agents of the supernatural, to prolong the life of the lost Poet. He becomes his sole mourner: 'ah! thou hast fled! / The brave, the gentle, and the beautiful, / The child of grace and genius' (688–90). But art and eloquence and even sobs and groans are vain 'when some surpassing Spirit, / Whose light adorned the world around it, leaves / Those who remain behind' (714–16). All that is left to us is 'pale despair and cold tranquillity, / Nature's vast frame, the web of human things' (718–19) – inadequate to our needs as they were inadequate to the Poet's – and 'Birth and the grave, that are not as they were' (720). Any judgement that we might have passed on the Poet, to the effect that he 'went too far' or failed to outgrow his adolescent narcissism, is brought up short by all this praise and grief. The naturally pious Narrator ends by railing against nature's limits.

So a good case can be made (there are many more details one could bring in) that *Alastor* presents two contrary standpoints, a natural and a supernatural, or an immanent and a transcendent, or a worldly and an otherworldly, and shows the limitations and uncertainties of each. If, as the Preface says, 'The picture is not barren of instruction to actual men', what the poem instructs us in is scepticism, an enlightened doubt as to which standpoint, if either, is true or right. The Preface, in fact, complicates this case, for it seems to side with the Narrator, and even goes beyond his view in using the language of vengeance, as we saw, implicit in Peacock's notion of an *alastor*: 'The Poet's self-centred seclusion was avenged by the furies of an irresistible passion pursuing him to speedy ruin.' A chief advocate of the sceptical-dialogue case even attributes the Preface to the Narrator, not to Shelley; that is, Shelley wrote it while adopting the mask of the Narrator, consciously or unconsciously, and we are not to take its opinions as gospel.

Against this case one may point out that it is a tricky business to separate the interpretations and judgements the Narrator may offer, implicitly in the poem or explicitly in the Preface, from the description of the Poet's life and death. To do so we must take the Narrator's word for the facts but bracket out his personal comments on the facts as inadequate. Are we to doubt the Narrator's assertion, for instance, that 'The spirit of sweet human love has sent / A vision to the sleep of him who spurned / Her choicest gifts' (203–5), because we saw nothing we could quite call spurning and because we dislike the idea that any 'spirit' other than the Poet's own imagining can exist? What really makes this passage less reliable than others, or in special need of correction? It is a little like the bottomless problem of the quest for the historical Jesus by means of the four Gospel texts alone; it is worse, because there is only one testimony concerning the Poet. Moreover we tend to ignore the contradiction at the heart of the poem: that much of the Poet's life, everything the Poet is quoted as saying, and above all his death had no witnesses! We might imagine the Narrator following the Poet's path and interviewing maidens, cottagers, and mountaineers, but the bulk of his story is either a supernatural revelation, unlikely for this naturalistic poet, or a fabrication.

The Narrator and the Poet have more in common, too, than the dialogue theory allows. The Narrator is also a poet, and we might note that he alone seems actually to have written anything. (Those critics who claim the Narrator's imagination is limited also neglect the evidence of his highly imaginative narration.) Like the Poet, the Narrator was fascinated with death. 'I have made my bed / In charnels and on coffins,' he tells us in the opening, 'where black death / Keeps record of the trophies won from thee' (23–5), hoping to force 'some lone ghost, / Thy messenger, to render up the tale / Of what we are' (27–9). He imagines himself trafficking in the supernatural in the closing passage as well, searching for an elixir of life, and he seems to believe in the story of the Wandering Jew (677–81). The Poet pursues the same interests as the Narrator, and seems to have gone one step farther; though the Mother has not yet unveiled her mysteries to the Narrator, the Poet does have a revelation into the 'secrets of the birth of time' (128) and, very equivocally, a vision of ideal love. Yet the Narrator also claims that 'Enough [of the mysteries] from incommunicable dream, / And twilight phantasms, and deep noonday thought, / Has shone within me' (39–41) that he feels ready to tell the story. This inner light is not a product of nature, it is not the usual inspiration of a nature poet.

It is also interesting that both Narrator and Poet, like their creator, are vegetarians. As a sign of his devotion to 'our great Mother' the Narrator claims 'no bright bird, insect, or gentle beast / I consciously have injured, but still loved / And cherished these my kindred' (13–15), while the Poet would linger in lonesome vales 'Until the doves and squirrels would partake / From his innocuous hand his bloodless food' (100–101).

There is an analogy that might be enlisted by both those who see the poets as fundamentally different and those who see them as much alike. The relationship between the Narrator and the Poet is similar to that between the Poet and his dream-maiden. The Poet is an ideal projection of the Narrator, and, while not explicitly erotic, the Narrator's feelings for the Poet are intense. As the loss of the maiden leads the desperate Poet to a passive suicide, the loss of the Poet leaves the Narrator in 'pale despair' (718), perhaps only a step from suicide himself. The difference, of course, is that the Poet dies, and the Narrator lives to write a poem about him. As the Poet dies, the Narrator likens him (among other things) to 'A fragile lute, on whose harmonious strings / The breath of heaven did wander' (667–8); that image echoes the one that begins the narrative: 'the charmed eddies of autumnal winds / Built o'er his mouldering bones a pyramid / Of mouldering leaves in the waste wilderness' (53–4). They both hearken to the conclusion of the opening, where the Narrator likens himself to 'a long-forgotten lyre' (42) awaiting the breath of the 'Great Parent' (45). That breath evidently comes, for the remarkable story gets told.

It has also been argued that Shelley did not, in the end, make it clear if we are to take *Alastor* as a sceptical dialogue or an anguished monologue, so we must be meant to take it as a second-order dialogue between these alternatives. In other words we are to be sceptical about scepticism! Occam's razor and common sense dictate that this idea is a non-starter, as well as a non-stopper, for it breeds an infinite regression. It seems wiser to allow that Shelley might not have sorted everything out properly than to elevate the seeming inconsistencies into a deliberate programme. Critics are always in search of a formula that would sublate, or simultaneously cancel and preserve at a higher level (as in Hegel's dialectic) all the contradictions of a text. *Alastor* in particular has attracted more commentary per line than any other poem of Shelley's, more than it deserves, no doubt, for few of the many commentators would rate it a great poem. But because it is the first long poem of Shelley's maturity it is important to try to understand it.

Wordsworth

If, as Mary Shelley wrote, *Alastor* reflects a turning away from his youthful concern with 'the present suffering, and what he considers the proper destiny, of his fellow-creatures', some of the other poems in the *Alastor* volume are much more public-spirited. The final poem, in fact, called *The Daemon of the World*, is a recasting of the first two cantos and last two cantos of *Queen Mab*. It thereby omits the most openly radical and subversive cantos, those that attack monarchy, war, commerce, and religion; it also tones down a few phrases in the cantos that remain. But Shelley does not conceal his scorn of tyranny and 'The bloodhound of religion's hungry zeal', and the vision of the future remains a social utopia, not an individualist retreat from society. Another poem, 'Superstition', is lifted out of canto VI of *Queen Mab* (lines 72–102), where it refers to 'religion'. It tells the history of superstition-religion, from belief in many gods invented by its 'frenzied brain' to a 'Baffled and gloomy' projection of the causes of all things back to a final cause, an 'abstract point', called 'God' (in the *Queen Mab* version). In his revision Shelley softens the conclusion by changing 'God' to 'name, and form, / Intelligence, and unity, and power', but a careful reader could hardly miss the argument that modern monotheism is but a mature version of ancient polytheism, both founded on ignorance.

Another poem in the *Alastor* volume, a sonnet whose title, 'Feelings of a Republican on the Fall of Bonaparte', announces clearly enough Shelley's political commitments, attacks Napoleon as a tyrant who deserved his defeat at Waterloo but attacks more sharply the 'legal Crime' of the victors (which of course included Great Britain) and the re-establishment of 'bloody Faith the foulest birth of time'.

Among three other sonnets, finally, is one that directly addresses the poet's proper mission in the world, 'To Wordsworth'.

> Poet of Nature, thou hast wept to know
> That things depart which never may return:
> Childhood and youth, friendship and love's first glow,
> Have fled like sweet dreams, leaving thee to mourn.
> These common woes I feel. One loss is mine
> Which thou too feel'st, yet I alone deplore.
> Thou wert as a lone star, whose light did shine
> On some frail bark in winter's midnight roar:
> Thou hast like to a rock-built refuge stood
> Above the blind and battling multitude:
> In honoured poverty thy voice did weave
> Songs consecrate to truth and liberty, –
> Deserting these, thou leavest me to grieve,
> Thus having been, that thou shouldst cease to be.

Wordsworth was the greatest poet of the generation just before Shelley's, the generation that came of age during the French Revolution and the widespread agitation in Britain. By the time Shelley came to read him, Wordsworth, like his friends Southey and Coleridge, had turned against France, republicanism, parliamentary reform, and the Godwinian philosophy he had once believed, and he was writing poems friendly to the Crown and Church of England. He accepted a government post in the county of Westmorland in 1813, the same year Southey became Poet Laureate and Leigh Hunt went to prison. In 1814 he published his long poem *The Excursion*; Shelley read it right away, and concluded, as Mary wrote in her journal, that 'He is a slave'.

As the sonnet makes clear, Shelley's respect for Wordsworth's early work was very great. In his themes of lost childhood and youth, lost friendship and love, Wordsworth spoke movingly to our common condition, and to Shelley's in particular; Shelley is alluding to some of the greatest of Wordsworth's poems, such as 'Tintern Abbey' and the 'Ode: Intimations of Immortality'. He exalts Wordsworth as unique and transcendent, as a 'lone star' whose light might save a frail bark – one of Shelley's distinctive images – from destruction, perhaps as an example to a younger poet trying to hold an even keel in a time of political reaction and despair. The older poet had sung freely and truly while in 'honoured poverty' ('modest means' would have been more accurate); now he has compromised himself and accepted his dishonourable government sinecure as Distributor of Stamps. The star has set, and Shelley is alone.

Until its last two lines this sonnet is a homage, and as is typical of a homage it pays tribute in a form characteristic of Wordsworth, who helped revive the use of the sonnet for public themes that we owe to Milton. Indeed Shelley seems to allude to Wordsworth's homage to Milton in 'London, 1802', which begins 'Milton! thou shouldst be living at this hour'. In that sonnet Shelley found the star image: 'Thy soul was like a Star, and dwelt apart: / Thou hadst a voice whose sound was like the sea: / Pure as the naked heavens, majestic, free'. Wordsworth himself may be alluding to Milton's own sonnet about his calling, 'When I consider how my light is spent'. In any event, by evoking the Miltonic sonnet tradition and Milton himself when he offers his own sonnet to Wordsworth, Shelley makes the abrupt reversal of the final lines all the more pointed and painful. It is as if he were saying, 'Wordsworth! thou shouldst be living at this hour', for they clearly imply his death; they are an elegy for a dead poet: 'thou leavest me to grieve, / Thus having been, that thou shouldst cease to be.' Strictly construed, the last line may mean: 'having been that kind of poet, that thou shouldst cease to be thus'; with the 'thus' placed at the front, however, the remainder of the line strongly implies the death of more than Wordsworth's principles.

The 'Songs consecrate to truth and liberty' should remind readers of that other song dedicated to 'knowledge and truth and virtue' and 'lofty hopes of divine liberty' sung by the dream-maiden in *Alastor* (158–9). The Poet awakes from that dream to the cold white light of morning and is marked by death thereafter, paying no heed to any other human being, including 'cottagers'. Is *Alastor* a kind of allegory or parable of Wordsworth, abandoned by the muse of truth and liberty, then dying a slow death, no longer sympathetic to the impoverished cottagers who were once his distinctive theme? Until recently many critics have interpreted it along these lines, taking the Poet as representing Wordsworth, or possibly Coleridge, but most critics now think that if anyone represents Wordsworth it is the Narrator, the poet of Nature. It is he who asks, right after the Poet awakes, 'Whither have fled / The hues of heaven that canopied his bower / Of yesternight?' (196–8) in an allusion, perhaps, to the famous question of the 'Intimations' ode: 'Whither is fled the visionary gleam? / Where is it now, the glory and the dream?' There are many other echoes of Wordsworth, including two distinct passages at the elegiac conclusion taken from the same ode. 'It is a woe too "deep for tears"' (713) is a quotation of the final line of the 'Intimations' ode, while the final line of *Alastor* is taken from a passage early in the ode: the things 'that are not as they were' (720) after the passing of the Poet remind us of the way things looked to Wordsworth after the passing of the 'celestial light' – 'It is not now as it hath been of yore'.

We might agree with the consensus that the Narrator is the more

Wordsworthian of the two, but the case is complicated by the analogy we proposed between the Poet and his dream-maiden on the one hand and the Narrator and his alter-ego Poet on the other. And that in turn points us to Shelley's situation. As he says in the 'Wordsworth' sonnet, he too feels the common woes that Wordsworth so memorably described, including the departure of 'love's first glow' (suggesting the dream-maiden, the Poet's first love), but he also shares another feeling of loss, Wordsworth's desertion of his calling as a poet. For Wordsworth that feeling may resemble the other griefs, but for Shelley, though he has not lost his radical social ideals, the feeling is doubled, for the poet who taught us how to deal with loss is now lost himself. The poet who had been a friend of humanity has now spurned it, and he leaves a younger poet, who would have hailed him as 'Brother' and 'friend' the way youthful maidens wrongly hailed the alienated Poet (269), alone and without a mentor.

3 'Mont Blanc'

Mont Blanc, on the border of France and Switzerland, is the highest peak in Europe. When Shelley saw it in 1816, it had recently been scaled, but it looked no less bleak, forbidding, terrifying, and 'awful' for that, as it still does to many travellers. His poem about it impresses many readers at first as a spontaneous and formless response to the mountain's overwhelming impression on the poet, as if it were simply a record of the 'legion of wild thoughts' the scene aroused (41). Shelley himself wrote that the poem 'was composed under the immediate impression of the deep and powerful feelings excited by the objects which it attempts to describe; and, as an undisciplined overflowing of the soul, rests its claim to approbation on an attempt to imitate the untamable wildness and inaccessible solemnity from which those feelings sprang.' It may indeed imitate that wildness and solemnity very effectively, but only because it is anything but an undisciplined overflowing of the soul: as we shall see, it is an artful, carefully conceived poem.

Just what kind of poem it is, if it belongs to a kind at all, is difficult to say, but the subtitle – 'Lines Written in the Vale of Chamouni' – gives us a clue, and so does the passage we have just quoted. Just as that passage echoes Wordsworth's famous definition of poetry as 'the spontaneous overflow of powerful feelings' in his Preface to the *Lyrical Ballads* of 1800, Shelley's subtitle evokes the greatest poem in *Lyrical Ballads*, 'Lines Composed a Few Miles above Tintern Abbey'. That poem is a model for what M.H. Abrams has defined as a new form of poetry, more or less invented by Wordsworth and Coleridge, 'the greater Romantic lyric': a speaker in a particular place outdoors, such as the banks of the Wye above Tintern Abbey, carries on a sustained colloquy with what he sees and with himself, beginning with a description of the scene and passing through memories and emotions into a meditation on the meaning of the scene or his life, often circling back to where he began with the outer description but in an altered mood and with deeper understanding. Such a poem's real subject is not the natural scene or objects but the meditation they prompt.

'Mont Blanc' is one of the most complex instances of this genre because its subject is in large part the very precondition of such poetry: the state of mind necessary for an 'unremitting interchange' (39) with the natural world, the belief that a single 'Power' governs both nature and the human mind, and the disturbing possibility that nature is vacant apart from the 'human mind's imaginings' (143). This subject is also related to the 'sublime', a category frequently treated during the eighteenth century in theoretical essays (by Edmund Burke and Immanuel Kant, among others) and in poetry and painting. Vast natural objects, such as a mountain, the sea, the night sky, or a thunderstorm, evoked feelings of wonder, terror, or religious awe as the mind of the observer tried to expand to take them in and understand them. This effort might lend a restless, even desperate intensity to the meditations typical of this Romantic genre, as it does for moments in 'Mont Blanc'.

Shelley's poem begins calmly enough, and rather surprisingly, not with a description of the mountain or its glaciers or rivers, but with an abstract philosophical statement about what we today would call the 'stream of consciousness'.

> The everlasting universe of things
> Flows through the mind, and rolls its rapid waves,
> Now dark – now glittering – now reflecting gloom –
> Now lending splendour, where from secret springs
> The source of human thought its tribute brings
> Of waters,   with a sound but half its own.
>
> (1–6)

The mind is a channel not only for thoughts (which arise from springs within the mind) but also for things, as if we were mainly passive blank slates on which the hand of experience writes, or mainly passive earth into which the river of experience has carved its valley. Yet we no sooner think of this Lockian model of the mind than we note that the entire universe flows through it, and that provokes the thought that perhaps the universe only exists in so far as it flows through it (a Berkeleyan or idealist model). That in turn raises the question as to whose mind this one is. Elsewhere Shelley posited the 'One Mind', a universal mind to which individual human minds contributed. I think this poem does not require us to distinguish two levels of mind; what it does demand is that we ponder the relationship between the mind – any mind – and the world it perceives and conceives.

We can imagine Shelley standing on the Pont Pellisier over the Ravine of Arve, while the river roars beneath him as he faces upstream, and feeling a kind of sensory overload as the torrent seems to come funnelling right into his eyes and ears. He soon muses that the river in its channel is much like our constant experience of the world. He then notes that he has been musing, and that his own thoughts form a stream themselves, as if in tribute to their object, which is the 'end' of the thoughts, as a river is the end of a tributary stream. He then contemplates the tributary idea further in a simile that is already implicit in the opening metaphor but which, like a Homeric simile, gives naturalistic detail that cannot be readily assigned to the mind.

> . . . with a sound but half its own.
> Such as a feeble brook will oft assume
> In the wild woods, among the mountains lone,
> Where waterfalls around it leap for ever,
> Where woods and winds contend, and a vast river
> Over its rocks ceaselessly bursts and raves.
>
> (6–11)

But these details may not really exceed the bounds of the comparison, for we already have the sense that the mind may be entirely at one with the universe. In a passage Shelley had recently read (quoted in the Preface to *The Excursion*), Wordsworth wrote that he would proclaim

> How exquisitely the individual Mind
> (And the progressive powers perhaps no less
> Of the whole species) to the external World
> Is fitted: – and how exquisitely, too –
> Theme this but little heard of among men –
> The external World is fitted to the Mind;
> And the creation (by no lower name
> Can it be called) which they with blended might
> Accomplish [.]

What two things could be more exquisitely fitted to each other than a river and its ravine? While it is true that the river over many aeons carved out the ravine, it is also true that the ravine now shapes the river, makes it the river that it is. And so the human mind might have mountains in it, and waterfalls, and rocks.

In any case, Shelley begins the second section with 'Thus' (12) and thereby redefines the whole of the first section as half of a large simile, the second half of which turns out to be the Ravine of Arve itself, directly addressed as 'thou'. Beyond its normal function as the marker of a simile, however, 'thus', so prominently placed, suggests 'therefore', as if Shelley has reversed the actual order of events, from perception of the real ravine and river to meditation on the ravine and brook of the mind and the river of the universe, and deduced the real ravine before him from his meditation. The process of the poem enacts, though it does not assert, a mental creation of the universe of things.

As a sustained apostrophe or address to the ravine, section II takes on some of the qualities of a Pindaric ode, which, as Abrams points out, was the form that the greater Romantic lyric more or less replaced. Simply to address something inhuman, the way classical poets in their odes addressed human beings or gods, is to bring the thing nearer, to humanize it, to raise the possibility of a conversation with it. And indeed in line 13 Shelley attributes voices to the vale, just as he has said the vast river 'raves', while in the third section he will attribute a tongue to the wilderness and a voice to the mountain (76, 80). To say 'thou' to a ravine or a mountain is a creative mental act, however commonplace it may be as a poetic figure, and Shelley is aware that in speaking to them and in writing of them in figurative language he is in some sense making them up. It is not the human mind that is the Lockian blank slate, he will suggest, but – in an implicit pun on its name – the mountain that is blank; or if not altogether blank, the natural world collaborates with the human mind and 'with blended might' they create reality.

Shelley even finds an example of such collaboration within the world of nature itself. There is a giant brood of pines

> in whose devotion
> The chainless winds still come and ever came
> To drink their odours, and their mighty swinging
> To hear – an old and solemn harmony [.]
>
> (21–4)

There would be no mighty swinging to hear, of course, if the winds did not come to hear it, and presumably no odours to drink if the winds did not elicit or scatter them. To find a case of subject–object interdependence within the realm of the object itself would seem to make Shelley's subjective view more objective! But of course Shelley has made it all up by attributing subjectivities to these objects, by personifying the winds and making them devotees of the trees. But again, this 'harmony' is produced by a kind of aeolian lyre, a frequent figure in Romantic poetry for the poet himself, in tune with nature and awaiting inspiration from it. In his 'Ode to the West Wind' Shelley will plead, 'Make me thy lyre, even as the forest is' (57). So we might take these winds and pines as a synecdoche for the entire natural scene before him, which inspires him into poetry, into this poem. He becomes the medium through which the natural world sings its song.

Early in the second part we meet the figure of 'Power', a monarch who comes down from his throne 'in likeness of the Arve' (15) as if it had decided to become a simile. It reminds us of the incarnations of Zeus in likeness of a swan or bull; in fact the Arve acts like Zeus' lightning bolt

(18–19). But the Arve must not be a very close likeness, for Power's throne is 'secret' (17), and later we learn 'Power dwells apart' and is 'inaccessible' (96–7). So described, this god inspires awe, and the possibility of human interchange with it seems remote, even though human thought also has a 'secret' source (4). As Shelley struggles throughout the poem to imagine the site of Power he can only see it as a desert, as a desolate inhuman waste, where the only human thing might be a hunter's bone brought there by an eagle (68). That may be a way of saying that Power is after all not like Zeus or any god, which are human creations in human likenesses; it is imageless, not part of the perceivable universe. If the mind is a ravine and the universe a river flowing through it, then Power is above or beyond the universe; if its seat is the peak of Mont Blanc, then it is the source of the universe-river: the snows no one beholds (131–2) produce the great glaciers (100f.) that melt into the Arve. Power then comes to resemble the ancient idea of the prime mover unmoved, the cause of all motion (but not the cause of all matter in an 'ever-lasting' universe), and indeed the principle of causality itself.

It is interesting that the only use of 'sublime' in the poem attaches not to the ravine or mountain but to the reverie or trance the ravine induces in Shelley.

> Dizzy Ravine! and when I gaze on thee
> I seem as in a trance sublime and strange
> To muse on my own separate phantasy,
> My own, my human mind, which passively
> Now renders and receives fast influencings,
> Holding an unremitting interchange
> With the clear universe of things around [.]
>
> (34–40)

It is this state of mind, as much as the natural surroundings, that impresses Shelley. 'Strange' is also an interesting adjective, as it suggests not only 'unusual' but also 'estranged' or 'alien' or, as in the next line, 'separate': the vertigo of the ravine seems to have split Shelley's mind in two, for the 'I' becomes detached somehow from the mind and contemplates it as an object. In speaking about this division, 'Shelley' (or what is left of him) contemplates both the I and the mind as his object, so there is an implicit third division and another I, and of course then a fourth division and a fifth and so on unto dizziness. What holds him together is precisely this trance, which suspends him in paradoxes, where a mind not only receives but 'passively . . . renders'. 'Influencings' is also a good word, for its context (a river) brings out its root meaning of 'flowing ins'.

The rest of this section is more difficult.

> One legion of wild thoughts, whose wandering wings
> Now float above thy darkness, and now rest
> Where that or thou art no unbidden guest,
> In the still cave of the witch Poesy,
> Seeking among the shadows that pass by
> Ghosts of all things that are, some shade of thee,
> Some phantom, some faint image; till the breast
> From which they fled recalls them, thou art there!
>
> (41–8)

This passage would seem to bear out Shelley's claim that the poem is an undisciplined overflowing of the soul, for many readers have disagreed over just what is going on here. The 'legion' seems to be in apposition to 'mind' and 'phantasy', which was the object of the musing I. As an object of a trance it ought to stand still, but this legion of thoughts wanders back and forth between the ravine ('thy darkness') and the cave of Poesy, as if it is really the musing I who thinks alternately of both ravine and mind. It is not clear, however, that we can take the cave as synonymous with the mind, for a cave is not a ravine. Indeed the Ravine of Arve has caverns of its own, as we are told twice (14, 30). So we may take this cave as a special part of the mind, a faculty or power. It is a little disconcerting to find a witch in it, but since this is the cave of Poesy, it is appropriate enough to find a figure from the old Spenserian 'romance' tradition where poetry was called 'poesy'. Unlike the 'caverns echoing to the Arve's commotion' (30) this cave is still, the place in the mind where 'that' (the legion, probably, but perhaps 'thy darkness') or 'thou' (43) (the ravine) is an invited guest and where the wandering thoughts rest after hovering over it. This legion of thoughts, 'wild' because it is wandering in the 'wilderness' (76), has lost its military discipline; it will find its commander, presumably, in the witch Poesy. Shelley was to use the same metaphor later, in *A Defence of Poetry*, where he writes that some poets created forms which, copied into men's imaginations, 'became as generals to the bewildered armies of their thoughts'.

Are we to conceive of Shelley back at his desk writing this poem, trying to summon up in his poem the ravine that so impressed him earlier in the day, but whose after-images are faint and ghostly, and therefore trying to conjure them into life as a witch would do? Or is he still standing on the bridge, and retreating into his brain (the cave as skull) to ransack his store of poetic imagery? Perhaps we should take 'poesy' as having the general sense of poetry in the *Defence*, 'the expression of the imagination', in which case what Shelley finds in this cave may be the tribute of human thought he names at the beginning (5), the influence that the mind renders (38) in the shaping of the total experience. If we think of Shelley at his desk, then the last clause (47–8) might mean simply that the ravine is before him as long as his wandering thoughts float above it or seek images of it in the cave. If he is still on the bridge, then his thoughts seem to have the radical power of constituting the very presence of the ravine, a power greater than the capacity for collaborative give-and-take we have assumed up till now; when the observer recalls the thoughts to his breast, breaking out of the trance, the ravine will vanish. It is hard to decide, then, just where 'there', the climactic word of the whole section, really is.

It is worth noting, by the way, that 'there' is the only end-word without a rhyme in section II. All the others find a rhyme, or more than one, though they may wait several lines before they do. For long stretches the verse avoids couplets or any regular pattern, and the effect is much like blank verse, which Wordsworth uses in 'Tintern Abbey' and *The Excursion*. We might call it 'blanc verse': it may 'imitate the untamable wildness' of what Shelley saw, but the good witch of poesy is at work, finding mates for all the end-words in his poem about that wildness. Even more interesting: in all of section IV there is only one unrhymed end-word, the very last, just as 'there' is the last of section II, and it is 'air'! Then the first line of section V ends with 'there', making a couplet straddling the stanza-break and reminding us of the long-unpartnered 'there' earlier. (Only two end-words in the entire poem, 'spread' at 65 and 'sun' at 133, never find rhymes – why I do not know.)

Whether he is still in his trance or not, Shelley abandons direct address to the ravine and only resumes it twice briefly to the mountain, at the ends of parts III and V (80–83 and 139–44). His tone seems less rapt, less excited, but his speculative thoughts are still floating about. If, as we have said, Power is above or beyond the perceivable universe, remote and inaccessible, then perhaps we can get an intimation of it when we are in a different state of mind, not so much in a trance as asleep, or even dead.

> Some say that gleams of a remoter world
> Visit the soul in sleep, – that death is slumber,
> And that its shapes the busy thoughts outnumber
> Of those who wake and live.

> (49–52)

Shelley's legion of thoughts was busy enough seeking images of the ravine, and the ravine corresponds to something human and (in part) knowable; those thoughts would fail, he implies, if they sought the mountain itself.

As the ravine-images they did seek were ghosts or shades, the thoughts have already entered the realm of death, as Odysseus and Aeneas went to speak with the shades in Hades. Now Shelley speculates that the shapes of death outnumber the thoughts of life, with the suggestion that if he could summon these shapes he would have a new legion for his assault on the mountain. As he looks on high, he wonders if he has entered this new and more profound condition that transcends mortal bounds: 'Has some unknown omnipotence unfurled / The veil of life and death?' (53–4) But his spirit fails, vanishing like a homeless cloud, as if his soul, too, had become a shade, a denizen of death.

That the veil is 'unfurled' has troubled some readers, for we would expect it to be 'furled' or raised, so that it no longer divides death from life. Earlier Shelley described the waterfall 'whose veil / Robes some unsculptured image' (26–27). That veil is surely unfurled; in fact the paradoxical phrase 'unsculptured image' foreshadows the descriptions of the indescribable Power itself, veiled from us by its very nature, at least while we are alive or awake. But Shelley went on to place a 'strange sleep' in apposition to 'veil', a sleep which 'Wraps all in its own deep eternity' (27–9) like 'the mightier world of sleep' in which he now imagines himself (55). He now feels wrapped (and rapt) in this mysteriously revelatory veil.

In contrast to the tumult of sight and sound of the ravine below, when Mont Blanc finally appears it is 'still, snowy, and serene'. It is then immediately set in contrast again to the 'subject mountains' and the glaciers, a realm of storms and hideous shapes and dead men's bones. Shelley returns to his speculations:

> Is this the scene
> Where the old Earthquake-daemon taught her young
> Ruin? Were these their toys? or did a sea
> Of fire envelope once this silent snow?
>
> (71–4)

No one answers, of course; no gleam from this remote world penetrates the merely human mind. The silence of the scene suggests that this attempt to posit a mythic personage (another female, like the witch) is itself a toy, a childish thing shrugged off by the wilderness.

So it is surprising that in the next passage, crucial to the poem, Shelley claims that the wilderness and mountains are teachers.

> The wilderness has a mysterious tongue
> Which teaches awful doubt, or faith so mild,
> So solemn, so serene, that man may be

But for such faith with nature reconciled,
Thou hast a voice, great Mountain, to repeal
Large codes of fraud and woe; not understood
By all, but which the wise, and great, and good
Interpret, or make felt, or deeply feel.

(76–83)

The lines about faith have caused no end of disputes among Shelley scholars. 'Faith' is almost always a pejorative term in Shelley's works. It refers to the religious superstitions, indeed the large codes of fraud and woe, which kings and priests have imposed on the ignorant for thousands of years and from which only a few souls, wise, great, or good, have freed themselves. It is not the sort of thing we expect this unknown omnipotence to be teaching. It makes much more sense that the mountain teaches 'doubt', the usual opposite of 'faith', and not much sense at all that it teaches both. Are we to imagine two sets of students, the doubters and the faithful, who learn contradictory lessons? If it teaches both doubt and faith, then this double-voiced Power is dubious indeed, and doubt can be the only lesson in the end.

Then there is the odd phrase 'But for such faith'. Does it mean that faith is an obstacle to reconciliation with nature? The manuscript shows that Shelley wrestled with this phrase more than with any other, trying 'with such a faith' and 'in such wise faith' before seeming to settle on 'in such a faith'. His intention at one point, then, was to present faith as the means, not the obstacle, to reconciliation with nature. But he authorized the phrase in the published version, which seems to mean the opposite. It is possible, if a little forced, to read 'but for such faith' as an intensified version of 'in such a faith'; 'but' can mean 'only', giving something like 'only by means of such faith'. I think this is what Shelley meant; reading it that way, in any case, makes the whole passage more coherent. But why is Shelley endorsing faith, and what about doubt?

'Mont Blanc' belongs to another literary context that we should consider here, a context less important than the greater Romantic lyric but decisive for the polemical edge of this poem. As a well-read English tourist in the Alps, Shelley was well aware of a century of previous English tourists who climbed the mountains in order to find the sublime – and God. In 1739 Thomas Gray and Horace Walpole made the grand tour, and Gray wrote to a friend, 'There are certain scenes [in the Alps] that would awe an atheist into belief, without the help of other arguments.' Other travellers said similar things, and in the visitors' albums of the French and Swiss inns Shelley could read their pious comments. In several of these albums, including the one in the inn near Mont Blanc, he directly defied this tradition by entering his occupation as 'atheist' (along with 'philanthropist' and 'democrat') in Greek. Later visitors saw these entries, of course, including the Poet Laureate, Robert Southey, and soon there was scandal back in England.

It is almost certain, too, that Shelley had a particular poem in mind, Coleridge's 'Hymn before Sun-Rise, in the Vale of Chamouni', which had appeared in two journals in 1802 and then again in Coleridge's own journal, *The Friend*, in 1809. Not only the subtitle, but several lines of the 'Hymn' echo in 'Mont Blanc'. It begins:

> Hast thou a charm to stay the morning-star
> In his steep course? So long he seems to pause
> On thy bald awful head, O sovran Blanc,
> The Arve and Arveiron at thy base
> Rave ceaselessly; but thou, most awful Form!
> Risest from forth thy silent sea of pines,
> How silently! Around thee and above
> Deep is the air and dark, substantial, black,
> An ebon mass: methinks thou piercest it,
> As with a wedge! But when I look again,
> It is thine own calm home, thy crystal shrine,
> Thy habitation from eternity!
> O dread and silent Mount! I gazed upon thee,
> Till thou, still present to the bodily sense,
> Didst vanish from my thought: entranced in prayer
> I worshipped the Invisible alone.

In both poems a river or rivers rave ceaselessly (11), 'silently!' follows another 'silent' or 'silently' (135–6), the mountain pierces the sky (60), and, most important, the poets 'gaze' on the scene until, 'entranced' or 'in a trance' (34–5), they encounter the 'Invisible'. At that point Coleridge stops thinking or imagining, falls to prayer, and devotes most of the remainder of his eighty-five lines to calling on the mountain and everything else in the scene to awaken and sing God's praises. In a nearly hysterical exclamation that must have made Shelley nauseous, Coleridge asks the objects before him who made them, and who arranged things the way they are. 'God!' he answers for them,

> God! let the torrents, like a shout of nations,
> Answer! and let the ice-plains echo, God!
> God! sing ye meadow-streams with gladsome voice!

Ye pine-groves, with your soft and soul-like sounds!
And they too have a voice, yon piles of snow,
And in their perilous fall shall thunder, God!

And as if this were not enough, in a prefatory note to his poem Coleridge wrote, 'the whole vale, its every light, its every sound, must needs impress every mind not utterly callous with the thought – Who *would* be, who *could* be an Atheist in this valley of wonders!'

Shelley answers that question for Coleridge with his own poem. Where Coleridge rests entranced in prayer, shutting down his usually endlessly speculative mind, Shelley begins his restless questioning. Where Coleridge and the whole tribe of pious gawkers found God, Shelley finds a witch, an Earthquake-daemon, and a mountain that repeals religious codes (unlike Mount Sinai, from which one of the worst codes was promulgated). Where Coleridge shouts out his 'Answer!' Shelley poses more and more questions, even at the very end of his poem. Where Coleridge, forgetting his own theories of the imagination, makes God the creator of everything, Shelley, truer to Coleridge's better self, makes the imagination joint creator with nature.

Where Coleridge has been reading the Psalms, finally, Shelley has been reading Lucretius. One of the inspirations of *Queen Mab*, as we saw, Lucretius' great Latin epic, *De Rerum Natura* or *On the Nature of Things* – whilh Shelley may echo with 'universe of things' twice (1, 40) and 'secret strength of things' once (139) – expressed the Epicurean philosophy of materialism and atomism in which there is no room for a Creator and in which nature, including mountains, has no purpose. The gods, which even in the Greek myths did not create the universe, are dismissed by Lucretius to a separate realm of serene irresponsibility and indifference to human cares. In *Queen Mab* Shelley combined the inherent laws of the material world with the indifferent gods into a 'Spirit of Nature! all-sufficing Power, / Necessity!' who 'Unlike the God of human error, . . . Requirest no prayers or praises' (VI.197–200); in 'Mont Blanc' the Power is described in Lucretian terms as it 'dwells apart in its tranquillity / Remote, serene, and inaccessible' (96–7).

I think the 'faith' that the wilderness teaches is not the noisy Christian faith of Coleridge, which is what Shelley elsewhere usually means by the word, but a different sort, which he carefully modifies: a 'faith so mild, / So solemn, so serene' (77–8), the latter two adjectives also attaching to the mountain or Power themselves (61, 97, 128). This faith is the same, or nearly the same, as the 'awful doubt' it is linked with, the 'or' suggesting that these are alternative ways of describing the same thing and not

47

radically different choices. An 'awful doubt' (77) is not mere scepticism or agnosticism but a religious atheism, an awe-filled doubt; 'awful', too, is used of the scene where Power is first named (15–16). Coleridge's faith is enough to make us give up on nature altogether, but Shelley's faithful doubt reconciles us to it. And lest we remain puzzled over this faith, Shelley distinguishes it in the next lines from the codes of fraud or woe, which the mountain, in its very silence, has the voice to repeal.

The mountain, as Shelley repeats in the next section, can 'Teach the adverting mind' (100), but it still requires human mediators to interpret it, make it felt, and feel it. It needs poets, in other words, who can write poems like 'Mont Blanc'. Much of the rest of the poem elaborates ideas stated in the first three sections, yet with the claims of poetry in mind we notice Shelley's continued efforts to find 'interpretations' of this inhuman scene. 'The glaciers creep / Like snakes that watch their prey' (100–101), he says, but we know that it is an error to attribute motives to inanimate nature. The formations on the glaciers seem to be a 'city of death', he says, but then withdraws the human metaphor: 'Yet not a city' (105–7). It is impossible, we sense, to find words for such a scene without resorting to animating and anthropomorphic terms. Rocks may 'have overthrown / The limits of the dead and living world' (111–13) but rocks are dead; we who are living can hope at most that a gleam of ultimate truth may visit us as we contemplate the scene in a trance. Any attempt to describe the scene as it really is, apart from human apprehension of it, seems to fall inevitably into a description of a scene that is hostile to human life, a scene from which human beings are explicitly absent: 'The race / Of man, flies far in dread; his work and dwelling / Vanish, like smoke before the tempest's stream, / And their place is not known' (117–20). That is not the same thing at all. It is the difference, perhaps, between mere vacancy and silence or solitude.

One might despair over this inevitable failure, but Shelley seems to say, and his poem seems to show in its very workings, that the effort too, is inevitable, and one of the glories of being human. Moreover, the Power works in us no less than in nature, acting as a guarantor of an ineffable affinity or interchange. 'The secret strength of things' governs both thought and the infinite dome of heaven (139–41), and each is incomplete without the other. The rather cryptic final question – 'And what were thou, and earth, and stars, and sea, / If to the human mind's imaginings / Silence and solitude were vacancy?' (142–5) – implies the answer given in the final word. All would be vacancy, all would be a blank, if the human imagination were unable to grasp silence and solitude. Silence and solitude may be inhuman in some sense, but their embodiment in the mountain (and earth, stars, and sea) teaches us what they are, teaches us something of their value to us. If the mind does not 'advert' to these great objects of nature, they will not exist in any meaningful sense, and we will grow vacant ourselves.

If Shelley has turned against Coleridge's pat theologizing, he has turned towards a passage he and Mary had recently read together, in her father William Godwin's memoir of her mother Mary Wollstonecraft. 'She found an inexpressible delight in the beauties of nature, and in the splendid reveries of the imagination. But nature itself, she thought, would be no better than a vast blank, if the mind of the observer did not supply it with an animating soul.'

Interpreting 'Mont Blanc' is a little like interpreting Mont Blanc: one could go on and on, sending ever fresh legions of thought up its flanks and never conquering it. Interpretation, however, is not all that is expected of us. The wise interpret the mountain's voice, but the great make it felt and the good feel it (82–3). At the outset we quoted Shelley's testimony that the ravine, the Arve, the glacier, and Mont Blanc stirred 'deep and powerful feelings' in him, that he wrote that poem under their immediate influence, and that the poem tries to imitate the wildness and solemnity – emotional qualities themselves – of the scene from which they sprang. We cannot recover Shelley's original feelings apart from the poem that may imitate them, but we can share the feelings of the speaker of the poem, whom we have out of convenience, but not in the end very misleadingly, been calling 'Shelley'. We may add his comment the following year, in his Preface to *The Revolt of Islam* (*Laon and Cythna*), that 'It is the business of the Poet to communicate to others the pleasure and the enthusiasm arising out of those images and feelings in the vivid presence of which within his own mind consists at once his inspiration and his reward.' If it were only an interpretation that he wished to communicate, he would not need to enlist 'the harmony of metrical language, the etherial combinations of the fancy, the rapid and subtle transitions of human passion, all those elements which essentially compose a Poem', but could write in prose. These essential elements of a poem are meant to arouse feelings in us.

It is difficult to write (in prose) about feelings in poetry, and literary criticism today is rightly scornful of the rhapsodic gush that used to pass for appreciations. Shelley did not share this scorn, however, and, if we wish to be 'good' readers of this 'great' poem, neither should we. Perhaps, after pencilling up our copies of the poem, Shelley would want us to throw it away, find a new copy, and take it with us as we wander off alone, or with a dear friend, into a woodland, where we sit by a brook and read the poem aloud, letting our feelings gush as they might. Shelley did not believe reason and emotion were separate: they were linked by the imagination, and by love.

4 'Hymn to Intellectual Beauty'

When Shelley was a scholar at Eton, or perhaps earlier at Syon House Academy, he had an emotional experience that he was to look back on as decisive for his vocation as poet and social reformer. This is how he describes it in his 'Dedication' to *Laon and Cythna* (1817):

> Thoughts of great deeds were mine, dear Friend, when first
>   The clouds which wrap this world from youth did pass.
> I do remember well the hour which burst
>   My spirit's sleep: a fresh May-dawn it was,
>   When I walked forth upon the glittering grass,
> And wept, I knew not why; until there rose
>   From the near school-room, voices, that, alas!
> Were but one echo from a world of woes –
> The harsh and grating strife of tyrants and of foes.
>
> And then I clasped my hands and looked around –
>   – But none was near to mock my streaming eyes,
> Which poured their warm drops on the sunny ground –
>   So without shame, I spake: – 'I will be wise,
>   And just, and free, and mild, if in me lies
> Such power, for I grow weary to behold
>   The selfish and the strong still tyrannise
> Without reproach or check.' I then controlled
> My tears, my heart grew calm, and I was meek and bold.
>
> And from that hour did I with earnest thought
>   Heap knowledge from forbidden mines of lore,
> Yet nothing that my tyrants knew or taught
>   I cared to learn, but from that secret store
>   Wrought linked armour for my soul, before
> It might walk forth to war among mankind [.]

Some biographers have questioned this tale as entirely or partly improbable, but I see no reason to doubt that something like it really took place; it is hard to see what Shelley would have gained by making it up. It also strikes some readers as a grandiose inflation of an overly sensitive boy's reaction to the petty cruelties of schoolmates and schoolmasters, but if the

51

Battle of Waterloo was won on the playing fields of Eton then it seems only right that the most dedicated champions of freedom, justice, and peace should take their vows there as well.

That is not to deny that Shelley may have recast the story to conform to a literary pattern. It is a little conversion narrative, in the tradition of Christian spiritual autobiography, though of course there is nothing explicitly Christian about it. It even echoes the prototype of all such narratives, the *Confessions* of St Augustine, from which Shelley had taken his epigraph to *Alastor*. For Augustine also wept uncontrollably one day, until there rose nearby, not the voices of harsh and grating strife, but the voice of a child singing; in reversing this detail Shelley neatly relocates the source of evil from one's own sinful nature, as Augustine believed was the case, to the tyranny of selfishness in the world. Augustine takes the child's song as a command to open the Bible and read the first passage he should find, and when he does so he finds: 'Not in revelling and drunkenness, not in lust and wantonness, not in quarrels and rivalries. Rather, arm yourselves with the Lord Jesus Christ'. Revelling and lust seem not to have been on Shelley's mind, but it was the sound of quarrels and rivalries, in part, that prompted his vow to arm himself in spiritual armour.

Seeing how Shelley rewrites the traditional conversion plot in *Laon and Cythna* alerts us to the implications of his earlier and briefer telling of the same incident in 'Hymn to Intellectual Beauty', which he composed just before or just after he wrote 'Mont Blanc'. That telling, however, makes up part of the structure of a 'hymn', the very name and form of which raise questions as to what Shelley was doing to the Christian tradition. In 'Mont Blanc', we saw, he is redeeming the mountain from its enslavement to pious Christian moralizing, such as he found in Coleridge, while in the 'Hymn', I shall argue, he is redeeming religion from Christianity, or redeeming the human spirit of Christianity from ossification and death. As a negative but all too typical example of what a hymn has come to be, Coleridge's 'Hymn before Sun-Rise' may have instigated Shelley's 'Hymn' as well as 'Mont Blanc'. Shelley may also have wanted to rescue the form of the hymn, then, from the church's grasp.

While thousands of Christian hymns had been published in the eighteenth century, the term 'hymn' could have a classical pagan connotation as well, as in the 'Homeric Hymns' to various gods and goddesses, several of which Shelley translated. In the eighteenth century, too, several hymns to personified abstractions appeared, such as Thomson's 'Hymn to Solitude' and Gray's 'Hymn to Adversity'. They are hardly distinguishable from odes. By calling it a hymn rather than an ode, however, Shelley suggests at the outset that he is inaugurating a new liturgy, and that 'Intellectual Beauty' is a new and worthier god.

What is 'intellectual beauty'? The phrase was in use among radical writers whom Shelley read, such as Mary Wollstonecraft, who contrasts a woman's 'beauty of features' with 'a fine woman, who inspires more sublime emotions by displaying intellectual beauty' (*A Vindication of the Rights of Woman*, Chap. 3). In his memoir of Mary Wollstonecraft, William Godwin confessed that, while he lacked 'an intuitive perception of intellectual beauty', Mary had this 'intellectual taste' in abundance. In his poem Shelley embraces these senses – a faculty of the mind, and the object or state perceived by such a faculty – under a larger category: it is the supernal power or source of both the faculty and its object, rather like the 'universal beauty' of Plato's *Symposium*, in Shelley's own translation two years later, the form of beauty itself, which subsumes and in some way underlies all particular instances of beauty. Here it is also a personification, and while Shelley is careful to refer to it as 'it' when not addressing it directly as 'thou' or 'thee', it is hard to resist the feeling that it is female, a goddess, and a fickle goddess at that, like Aphrodite, who must be implored to stay constant. It also somewhat resembles the Muse because, as we shall see, it has much to do with poetry.

Shelley may have wanted to make another point, having to do with the standard contrast between the beautiful and the sublime. The sublime, as we can infer from 'Mont Blanc', is 'awful' or awesome, rugged, vast, astonishing, not fully comprehensible to the mind, and masculine, while the beautiful is pleasing, delicate, elegant, not too large, capable of appreciation by the viewer without strain, gentle, and feminine. Taken together, the 'Hymn' and 'Mont Blanc' might seem to be Shelley's attempt to embody the two categories. And yet the opening line of the 'Hymn', 'The awful shadow of some unseen Power', raises the possibility that Intellectual Beauty is sublime. In an earlier version, which survives in manuscript in Mary's hand, the poem begins: 'The lovely shadow of some awful Power'. Shelley seems to have been trying to relate the categories ontologically, the sublime being the higher origin of the beautiful, as if Shelley had felt he had omitted the beneficent side of the Power in 'Mont Blanc'. In the published version of the 'Hymn', we are not certain at first whether Intellectual Beauty is the shadow or the Power, but it is in either case sublime. Twice later it is addressed as 'awful': 'Unknown and awful as thou art' (40) and 'O awful LOVELINESS' (71); once 'some sublimer world' is mentioned (25), perhaps the Power's home. Addison had commented that parts of *Paradise Lost* are beautiful because they are sublime, implying that the beautiful is the larger category; Shelley may have first tried to reverse the hierarchy and then decided to make the distinction collapse altogether. And he may have been thinking of Mary's mother's point that intellectual beauty inspires 'more sublime emotions'.

> The awful shadow of some unseen Power
>> Floats though unseen amongst us, -- visiting
>> This various world with as inconstant wing
> As summer winds that creep from flower to flower.
> Like moonbeams that behind some piny mountain shower,
>> It visits with inconstant glance
>> Each human heart and countenance;
> Like hues and harmonies of evening, --
>> Like clouds in starlight widely spread, --
>> Like memory of music fled, --
>> Like aught that for its grace may be
> Dear, and yet dearer for its mystery.

(1–12)

Is it pressing the point too far to say that this stanza form is beautiful rather than sublime? A sublime form might be that of 'Mont Blanc', with 'stanzas' varying in length, lines randomly rhymed, and long grammatical periods sustained at high rhetorical pitch. The 'Hymn' stanza form, which seems to be Shelley's invention, never varies in its seven appearances, as if it were set to the same liturgical music. And very musical it is. The frequent repetition of words – 'unseen', 'visiting/visits', 'inconstant', 'flower to flower', 'dear, and yet dearer' – seems motivated as much by music as by sense, as if the whole stanza were a 'memory of music fled'. There is a running alliteration on initial vowels, through 'awful', 'unseen', 'amongst us', 'inconstant', and 'evening', to its climax in 'aught', as well as the more obvious clusters around *m* and *h* sounds. The five short lines (eight syllables) form two couplets and half the final couplet, while the latter three, in the first stanza, are anaphoric, all beginning with 'Like'. The fifth line of each stanza is an alexandrine (twelve or thirteen syllables), making the first five lines rather like the last five lines of a Spenserian stanza, several hundred of which Shelley was soon to compose for *Laon and Cythna*. As the theme of the poem is the inconstancy of Intellectual Beauty, the constancy of the highly wrought stanzas embodies a counter-theme, as if they are lures or gilded cages to capture the elusive awful Beauty. Shelley will do something similar in his great 'Ode to the West Wind'.

Four of the five concrete similes for the 'shadow' in the opening stanza are drawn from nature: summer winds, moonbeams, hues and harmonies of evening, and clouds in starlight. These and some of the later natural comparisons have led some readers to argue that Intellectual Beauty visits nature as well as the human mind, incarnating itself in natural beauty. But these similes are only similes; they are analogues for an event in the human intellect that cannot be described literally. It floats 'amongst us' and visits 'This various world' (the manuscript has 'This peopled world') and 'Each human heart and countenance'. Only its analogues visit nature. In fact the very number of analogues suggests that none of them comes very close to grasping the mystery, and the last one, 'Like aught', is a desperate catch-all category (repeated in the second stanza). They all share the trait of inconstancy or evanescence, but one is invisible and three are visible, two are light and one is a barrier to light, and so on. In his philosophical speculations Shelley was to argue that the distinction between mind and matter, or thought and thing, was superficial, and that all our perceptions of natural things are events in the mind. Whether you are a materialist or an idealist is less important than whether you are a monist or a dualist. In the end, then, natural events may bear a deep kinship to mental ones, but one must not merge them prematurely, especially in reading a poem which, like 'Mont Blanc', raises questions about the human connection with the universal power.

The second stanza begins by reiterating that it is human thought or form and not nature that the spirit of Beauty visits, but then dwells on the brevity of those visits:

> Spirit of BEAUTY, that dost consecrate
>> With thine own hues all thou dost shine upon
>> Of human thought or form, – where art thou gone?
> Why dost thou pass away and leave our state,
> This dim vast vale of tears, vacant and desolate?
>>> Ask why the sunlight not forever
>>> Weaves rainbows o'er yon mountain river,
> Why aught should fail and fade that once is shewn,
>>> Why fear and dream and death and birth
>>> Cast on the daylight of this earth
>>> Such gloom, – why man has such a scope
> For love and hate, despondency and hope?
>
> (13–24)

Its visits are brief, and its departures leave us desolate, far more desolate, one would think, than the commonplace fading of rainbows leaves rainbow-lovers, though rainbows traditionally symbolize hope and a covenant with the divine. This stanza asks two questions – Where art thou gone, and why? – and then answers them, as if in another voice, by posing four more; if we could answer these, presumably, we could answer those. But there is no answer to any of them. It is in the nature of man to be blown this way and that by his own inconstant feelings, and to find no certainty of belief no matter where he turns, for

> No voice from some sublimer world hath ever
>> To sage or poet these responses given –
>> Therefore the name of God and ghosts and Heaven,
> Remain the records of their vain endeavour,
> Frail spells – whose uttered charm might not avail to sever,
>> From all we hear and all we see,
>> Doubt, chance, and mutability.
> Thy light alone – like mist o'er mountains driven,
>> Or music by the night wind sent
>> Through strings of some still instrument,
>> Or moonlight on a midnight stream,
> Gives grace and truth to life's unquiet dream.

> (25–36)

Moses' claim that he heard the voice of God was a fraud designed to enforce his new code on the people, and Mont Blanc is the answer and antitype to Mount Sinai. Mont Blanc, we saw, has a voice to repeal large codes of fraud and woe but not a voice to ordain a new one, though in its very silence it can teach serene faith and awful doubt. No voice from a transcendent realm has ever answered anyone's questions, and it is only our own voice we hear as we vainly try by religious formulas to separate this world from doubt, chance, and mutability. The formulas are mere names: 'God' to suppress our doubts, 'ghosts' and 'Heaven' to convince us that there is a 'sublimer world' than this one, free of chance and change, where we go after death, but all of the names are as powerless as the spells or charms of a magician. Atheist Shelley is again showing his colours, and at this point his editor Leigh Hunt seems to have got nervous. The first published version, in the *Examiner* (1817), read 'Demon' for 'God', though 'Heaven' remained. Shelley, however, must have enjoyed coming up with the perfect substitute for 'God'!

If the 'Hymn' is an attack on orthodox Christianity, it borrows from Christianity many of its terms for Intellectual Beauty. In the final simile of the first stanza Beauty is likened to anything with 'grace' and 'mystery'; in the next it consecrates all that it shines upon; it lends 'grace' again in the third. Even the restriction of its visits to the human and not the natural world agrees with Christian doctrine. Shelley wants to preserve something of the human attitude or feeling of a believing Christian without the belief itself, as if, like many Christian reformers before him, he sought an original pure Christianity beneath the centuries of priestly codification of fraud and woe. In this he most resembles the 'Holy Ghost' Christians, like the Quakers and Ranters of seventeenth-century England, or like his contemporary William Blake. Among such Christians the Father and the Son are not given much weight, as they seem at best secondary theological formulas; it is the third person of the Trinity that makes us Christians: Christ in us, the Inner Light, the spirit of community and love.

It is this preservation of some human essence beneath the false accretions that makes Shelley a Romantic, in the end, rather than an Enlightenment *philosophe* like Godwin or Paine or Volney. He agreed with their demolition of superstition, but did not include under the rubric of superstition the reachings of the human imagination towards a realm that would answer the disparity between the soul and the 'dim vast vale of tears' (another quasi-biblical phrase) in which it must dwell. T.E. Hulme could have cited Shelley's 'Hymn' as an example of his scornful but brilliant definition of romanticism as 'spilt religion', but he seems to have missed the extent to which Christianity itself is constantly spilling out of the transcendent containers the priests try to confine it to, not least at the first Pentecost, when the Holy Ghost descended on the faithful. All conversion experiences, including the one Shelley records, are descents of the Spirit. If his seems to be an anti-conversion, as we shall see shortly, it is also a true conversion to a higher, if less comforting, religion.

If Shelley is establishing a truer or higher form of Christianity, we see in the next stanza that he must replace one of the three cardinal virtues, faith, with one that suits this human world.

> Love, Hope, and Self-esteem, like clouds depart
>   And come, for some uncertain moments lent.
>   Man were immortal, and omnipotent,
> Didst thou, unknown and awful as thou art,
> Keep with thy glorious train firm state within his heart.
>   Thou messenger of sympathies,
>   That wax and wane in lovers' eyes –
> Thou – that to human thought art nourishment,
>   Like darkness to a dying flame!
>   Depart not as thy shadow came,
>   Depart not – lest the grave should be,
> Like life and fear, a dark reality.
>   (37–48)

The subjunctive 'were' in the third line makes it clear that man's heart cannot sustain the firmness that would allow Intellectual Beauty to rule or keep state, but even if his heart could do so, we may wonder how it would make man immortal and omnipotent. Godwin and Condorcet had speculated on the indefinite prolongation of human life, but Shelley may be taking immortality and omnipotence in a 'subjective' sense, at least to the extent that subject and object can be distinguished in his philosophy. In a note to *Queen Mab* he argued that if 'the human mind, by any future improvement of its sensibility, should become conscious of an infinite number of ideas in a minute, that minute would be eternity'. This fascinating idea itself needs more explanation than Shelley gives it, but it suggests that, however long one lives, if one lives with great intellectual intensity, that life will be eternal and omnipotent enough. As he goes on to say in the note, with what we now see as a tragic poignancy, 'the life of a man of virtue and talent, who should die in his thirtieth year, is, with regard to his own feelings, longer than that of a miserable priest-ridden slave, who dreams out a century of dulness.'

This firmness, this receptivity, waxes and wanes, however, as Shelley has been showing us over several stanzas through many natural similes. In this stanza one of them is rather startling: Beauty nourishes human thought as darkness nourishes a dying flame. We have been thinking of Beauty as bright or shining (14) and several similes for it are light-filled, such as moonbeams, sunlight, and rainbows, whereas our ordinary life is a 'dark reality' (48) or a 'gloom' (23) cast on daylight. Here it is human thought that shines, though it is dying, and Beauty that is darkness, though a darkness that gives thought life. (Shelley is probably invoking more than an optical effect here, for some scientists in his day held that strong light could actually stifle a flame.) This image only takes to an extreme, however, the darker side of Intellectual Beauty, which is called 'shadow' three times (1, 46, 59) and likened to clouds and mist in other similes. It is not, then, a figure of enlightenment so much as a figure of contrast to our ordinary minds, which need enlightenment, to be sure, but also need the deeper if more elusive force of Beauty, which like many great paintings is a creature of *chiaroscuro*, or light and shade.

That Shelley should plead with Beauty to 'depart not' (46, 47) even though he knows perfectly well that it must do so expresses all the more vividly what is at stake. A visitation of Intellectual Beauty is much more intense than an ordinary aesthetic experience, at a concert hall, for instance, though music is one of the similes for it. While the visitation is taking place it is so powerful an enchantment that it alone feels like life, and its departure marks so steep a fall that the aftermath feels like death. Two utterly different orders of experience are in play, each convincing enough to claim to be reality in the absence of the other. The motive behind this sharp and emotional contrast, it seems, is a fear of literal death – the fear that death might be a final reality and not, as Queen Mab promised Ianthe, and the Poet of *Alastor* desperately hoped, a gateway to a 'sublimer world'. It is as if the very experience that evinces the possibility of such a world so alienates us from this world that the fact that it is merely a possibility becomes excruciating.

Yet as a boy, we learn, Shelley was already obsessed with death and the hope of a realm on the other side of it.

> While yet a boy I sought for ghosts, and sped
>   Through many a listening chamber, cave and ruin,
>   And starlight wood, with fearful steps pursuing
> Hopes of high talk with the departed dead.
> I called on poisonous names with which our youth is fed;
>   I was not heard – I saw them not –
>   When musing deeply on the lot
> Of life, at that sweet time when winds are wooing
>   All vital things that wake to bring
>   News of buds and blossoming, –
>   Sudden, thy shadow fell on me;
> I shrieked, and clasped my hands in extacy!
>
> (49–60)

Here is the retelling of the boyhood experience he was to enlarge on in *Laon and Cythna*. Out of context we might take the first four lines as concerning the sort of thing that fills gothic novels (and the sort of thing we know Shelley did as a boy) – spending nights in graveyards or ruins, chanting magic spells to conjure ghosts – like the Narrator of *Alastor*, who slept in charnel-houses and tried to force some ghost to tell the tale of what we are, or the mind in the cave of the witch Poesy in 'Mont Blanc', who sought the ghost of the ravine. But as the similar scene of Stanza 3, where the 'charm' of 'frail spells' has no effect, was really about orthodox Christian doctrine, we are invited to interpret this scene in the same way. The 'poisonous names' must refer to 'God or ghosts and Heaven', names fed him by priests in catechism class or by pious parents at home. The original manuscript reading, 'I called on that false name with which our youth is fed: / He heard me not', brings out the main anti-Christian point more clearly, but in changing 'false' to 'poisonous' Shelley not only makes better use of 'fed' but he may have been trying to link the graveyard setting to the church itself, as if to say that the religious categories we learn at church dry up the channels of our life and turn us deathward.

It is at the time of life's renewal, in any case, that Beauty's shadow fell on the boy. The metaphorical winds that creep from flower to flower (4) or send music through the strings of an instrument (33–4) are here made actual on a spring day, where they woo 'All vital things', including the boy, with 'News' – which may remind us of the 'Good News' or Gospel that Jesus rose from the dead on another spring day – 'of buds and blossoming'. (Some editions of Shelley still print 'birds and blossoming', but 'buds' is surely what he wrote.) This vernal breeze, which we shall meet again in 'Ode to the West Wind', seems more than an analogue here. In the final stanza Shelley suggests it is 'the truth of nature' (78–9). If it is not itself the movement of the Spirit, it seems to elicit the state of ecstasy or rapture which marks the turning point or conversion of Shelley's life and the climax of the poem.

The sudden visitation of Intellectual Beauty made the boy a new kind of priest:

> I vowed that I would dedicate my powers
>> To thee and thine – have I not kept the vow?
>> With beating heart and streaming eyes, even now
> I call the phantoms of a thousand hours
> Each from his voiceless grave: they have in visioned bowers
>>> Of studious zeal or love's delight
>>> Outwatched with me the envious night –
> They know that never joy illumed my brow
>>> Unlinked with hope that thou wouldst free
>>> This world from its dark slavery,
>>> That thou – O awful LOVELINESS,
> Wouldst give whate'er these words cannot express.

> (61–72)

He is also a new kind of magician. As a boy he had tried to conjure ghosts or the departed dead, and now he summons up from their graves the phantoms of a thousand hours. The point of this metaphorical conjuring, of course, is not to question the phantoms of past time but to present them as witnesses before Intellectual Beauty, before whom he is pleading his case that he, for his part, has been faithful. As for his duties, 'studious zeal' sounds fitting enough for a traditional priest, but 'love's delight' keeps before us the idea that this is a new religion. Though Jesus also preached brotherly love, the church that has spoken in his name for centuries has practised very little of it, and the time has come for a new gospel of love. Only that gospel might free the world from its 'dark slavery'. Shelley will go forth like one of the apostles to enlighten the heathen.

And how will he preach? Presumably by poetry. It was 'sage or poet' who listened for voices from the higher realm (26) and so perhaps a new kind of poet will spread the word about Intellectual Beauty. The many hours of 'studious zeal' might well refer to the labour of writing poetry. What is Intellectual Beauty, then, if not the muse? When Shelley invokes it, or pleads with it not to depart, he speaks as if his poem itself might speak, a poem that comes into being as Beauty approaches – the first line names its creator, as it were, even as it is being created – and may dissolve as Beauty departs. The anxious endeavour of Shelley the speaker to keep the spirit of Beauty firmly in his heart is a figure for the effort of the poem to keep itself going, a *tour de force* not quite on the scale of 'Mont Blanc' but faced with a similarly elusive and doubtful subject.

The stanza ends with two hopes. The social hope that the enslaved world might be free may have something in common with the personal hope that Beauty might 'give whate'er these words cannot express.' By naming this 'whatever', another catch-all term like the 'aughts' and 'alls' of earlier stanzas, Shelley tries to express the inexpressible, pointing to something that he cannot say. But of course what his words have been trying to express all along is precisely Intellectual Beauty itself. To ask it to express itself is both to confess the inadequacy of poetry 'in the letter' (in St Paul's famous phrase) and to proclaim the power of poetry 'in the spirit' to liberate the world. It is to ask to be freed from bondage to the literal terms of orthodoxy. The letter kills, it is poisonous; the spirit gives life. Poetry, by 'deliteralizing' the traditional terms, by recasting them through many transient similes, can evoke or embody if not quite express the truth that is indistinguishable from Beauty.

Some sort of crisis seems to have passed with the sixth stanza, and the seventh brings a very different mood.

> The day becomes more solemn and serene
>   When noon is past – there is a harmony
>   In autumn, and a lustre in its sky,
> Which through the summer is not heard or seen,
> As if it could not be, as if it had not been!
>   Thus let thy power, which like the truth
>   Of nature on my passive youth
> Descended, to my onward life supply
>   Its calm – to one who worships thee,

> And every form containing thee,
> Whom, SPIRIT fair, thy spells did bind
> To fear himself, and love all human kind.
>
> (73–84)

The afternoon he describes may remind us of the 'faith so mild, / So solemn, so serene' that the mysterious tongue of Mont Blanc may teach. The mysterious Intellectual Beauty has taught him the same calm faith, he claims, and he asks it to keep its initial lesson firm in his heart. Shelley borrowed the tone and attitude of this stanza from Wordsworth, in particular his 'Intimations' ode (as he had borrowed phrases from it in *Alastor*), and it might be interesting for the reader to consider the 'Hymn' in the light of that ode. Light, in fact, is the major image they share, including the contrast between the celestial light or cloud of glory and the common light of day. The 'philosophic mind' (187) that lets Wordsworth look calmly through the 'setting sun' (197) and 'man's mortality' (199) may have a stronger presence in Shelley's conclusion than the progress of his hymn leads us to expect, with its anxious questions and pleadings, but then it is only appropriate that it should be another poem, an embodiment of Intellectual Beauty, that supplies its calm to this one.

We might note in passing that Shelley does not limit the imagery for Beauty to the visual, as Wordsworth did. He is careful to pair things seen with things heard: 'hues and harmonies of evening' (8); 'clouds in starlight' followed by 'memory of music' (9–10); mist, music, and moonlight together (32–5); and 'harmony' and 'lustre' here at the end (74–5). He spells out the perceptual world as 'all we hear and all we see' (30), repeats that pairing in the boyhood scene – 'I was not heard – I saw them not' (54), and returns at the end with the harmony and lustre which is not 'heard or seen' in summer (76). This punctiliousness would imply something important. We have seen that music accompanies Shelley's utopias and visionary moments, if we may still call them visionary and not auricular; now we may see another motive in the connection between Intellectual Beauty and poetry that we just mentioned. Poetry, to Shelley, is more like music than painting or natural scenery, and all the more so if it is taken in its spiritual sense, as shadowing forth what it cannot put in words, expressing the inexpressible like the shadow of the mysterious power itself.

The poem concludes with another correction of Christian doctrine, another Romantic 'spilling' of transcendent religious categories into the immanent world of human beings. God himself said, 'the fear of the Lord, that is wisdom' (Job XXVIII.28), and the Bible echoes it in many places. 'Fear God, and keep his commandments,' says Ecclesiastes (XII.13), 'for this is the whole duty of man.' For Shelley, wisdom and duty begin with 'Love, Hope, and Self-esteem' (37), not obedience to a poisonous God. The 'fear' he mentions twice (21 and 48) becomes transfigured at the end into the respect or reverence for oneself from which true spiritual life and true love of humankind arise.

5   *Prometheus Unbound*

When Shelley reported to his tutor at University College, Oxford, in the autumn of 1810, he was given his first Greek reading assignment: Aeschylus' *Prometheus Bound*. How quickly he grasped its imaginative possibilities we may wonder, for his first discussion of Prometheus, in the note to *Queen Mab* about vegetarianism, is more ingenious than profound, and is not original with him. It also relies on older versions of the myth by Hesiod, from whom Aeschylus differs on several points. Hesiod's liver-eating eagle, for example, is found in *Prometheus Bound* only as a threat announced by Hermes at the end of the play, a new torture if Prometheus fails to reveal his fatal secret about Zeus. We can assume it was a more careful reading of the play, sometime after writing *Queen Mab*, that led Shelley to abandon the vegetarian allegory as too feeble to impose on the Aeschylean struggle between the king of the gods and the benefactor of humankind, and there is no trace of it in Shelley's play. (Peacock made good sport of the vegetarian allegory in his 1816 novel *Headlong Hall*.) Shelley eventually came to see the Prometheus legend as the mythical form of his own most cherished beliefs about the power of enlightenment over superstition, of stoic patience and hope over tyrannical violence, of the human over the divine, and he was to fold into it something not found in the original, his faith in the power of love and forgiveness over hatred and revenge.

Shelley was not the first to draw out these themes. Among ancient gnostic allegorists, for instance, Prometheus was seen as a 'philosopher' superior to fate, one who spurned the gifts and threats of Zeus, just as gnostic Christians spurned the false god Jehovah and tried to rise above the world he governs. Orthodox Christians interpreted Prometheus as a rebel like Lucifer against the high god, though it was also possible to take Prometheus as a type of Christ crucified by a satanic Zeus; Shelley was to deploy both of these readings. In the eighteenth century Prometheus sometimes appears as the patron god of the Enlightenment, indeed the god of atheism, notably in Goethe's early poem and play. In the poem (1773), Prometheus scornfully addresses the Olympians:

> I know of nothing under the sun, Gods,
> More miserable than you!
> You wretchedly feed
> Your majesty
> On tithe-offerings
> And prayer-breath,
> And you'd starve
> If children and beggars
> Weren't hope-filled fools.

Goethe probably did not know Aeschylus' play, but he saw the radical anti-religious germ in the stories of Hesiod. The *Theogony* tells of a dispute between gods and mortals at Mecone, where Prometheus tricks Zeus into choosing the inferior portion of a sacrificed ox so that humans can eat the bulk of the meat. Angry at the trick, Zeus withholds fire from humans, presumably so they cannot roast their meat, but Prometheus steals it for them, whereupon Zeus punishes him by having him bound to a column as prey to the hungry eagle (who unlike humans can eat meat raw). This story may indeed have something to do with the establishment of meat-eating, as Shelley first claimed, but it has more to do with the rules of sacrifice. Prometheus threatens not only the tithe-rights of the gods but also in a sense their very existence, for once humans learn they can outwit the gods they are only a step from thinking their way out of believing in them altogether. Of course, those who administer the sacrificial rites, the priests, simultaneously manipulate the gods, by extracting promises in return for offerings, and the mortals, by extracting offerings in return for promises. But the memory of Prometheus is latent atheism: we, too, may defy the gods and their agents, though at the risk of an *auto-da-fé*.

There is another myth, not in Hesiod but presumably just as old, that Prometheus was the creator of the human race; like the God of the Old Testament, he fashioned them of clay – Prometheus was the god of potters at Athens. Goethe makes use of this myth in his play, and so does Beethoven in his ballet *The Creatures of Prometheus* (1801). It is in a way superfluous, however, to the better known story of the gift of fire, for it is fire, and the technology that it makes possible, that raises humans above the level of beasts (and indeed enables humans to eat beasts). Fire may be taken as a synecdoche for culture, for language, for thought. In Aeschylus' play Prometheus tells how 'I found them [mortals] witless and gave them the use of their wits'; they had lived like ants in the ground, ignorant of time and season, until he taught them astronomy, writing, counting, taming of animals, horsemanship, navigation, metallurgy, and all the rest of the civilized arts, making them truly human. This idea, too, is central to Shelley's play.

When Shelley the student was assigned to read *Prometheus Bound* an Aeschylus revival was reaching its peak in England. The first English translation of any Aeschylus play was Thomas Morrell's 1773 version of *Prometheus in Chains*, which Morrell claimed to be the 'first play extant', the oldest surviving drama in western literature; several translations of the seven extant plays soon followed, and in 1809 and 1810 both Oxford and Cambridge were producing texts, commentaries, and public debates on Aeschylus. More important to Shelley, perhaps, was the increasingly common use of Prometheus as a symbol of enlightenment, of resistance to tyranny, of republicanism, even of America and George Washington. The American Joel Barlow's epic poem *The Columbiad*, published in London in 1809, makes several allusions to Prometheus as the spirit of enlightened freedom in America. In that same year a commemorative volume was issued with the title *Poems on the Abolition of the Slave-Trade*; it contains an engraving of 'Prometheus Delivered by Hercules' and a poem explaining it as an allegory of the liberation of the African race by the 'friend of man', the philanthropists of England. Shelley might well have seen it at home, for his father had voted for abolition in 1807.

Like Shelley, Byron had studied *Prometheus Bound* in school and even translated a bit of it. He mentions Prometheus over a dozen times in his poems, and in 1816, while he was with Shelley in Switzerland, he wrote his ode 'Prometheus'. There the Titan, a defiant stoic, is 'a symbol and a sign / To Mortals of their fate and force': in him man can foresee 'His wretchedness, and his resistance', his own strength of will to stand firm against 'his sad unallied existence' that ends in death. To Shelley this would have appeared heroic but one-sided, for there is no future, no hope, no possibility of breaking the cycle of punishment, defiance, and further punishment. But to Byron Shelley 'talked utopia'.

Whenever it was that Shelley began a serious study of *Prometheus Bound*, he would have found not only Byron's noble despair, but hints of something much worse. Aeschylus' play begins with the chaining and impaling of Prometheus to the rock by Zeus's agents Hephaestus, Force, and Violence. After a monologue from Prometheus complaining of his unjust punishment, a chorus of Oceanides (Ocean nymphs) arrives, and

Prometheus tells them of the war between the Olympians and the Titans in which he, though a Titan, sided with the Olympians. But he defied Zeus's plan to obliterate the human race, and he gave it fire. For such defiance he is tortured on the rock. Ocean appears, offering to mediate if Prometheus will yield; Prometheus haughtily refuses. He recites to the chorus all his gifts to humankind. Then Io, in the form of a cow, suddenly rushes in, pursued by a gadfly, and tells how she has been punished by Zeus for refusing his overtures. Prometheus tells of her future sufferings, of his own eventual release by her descendant Heracles (Hercules), and of secret knowledge he has of a fatal marriage Zeus will make unless he warns him. He repeats his prediction of Zeus's downfall to the chorus and to Hermes, who is sent by Zeus to extract the secret. Prometheus defies all threats, and the play ends amid earthquake and thunderstorm. Nothing has been accomplished in this nearly actionless play but an intensification of the stalemate between two immortals; Prometheus' final lines, invoking mother earth and the circling sky to witness how he suffers, nearly repeat the first lines of his opening speech.

This plot would seem to bear out Byron's view of Prometheus as a figure of tragic resignation, but Shelley was interested in the fact that the play was only one third of a trilogy, three plays performed together at the tragic festival, like the three plays of Aeschylus' *Oresteia*. The other two have been lost, but we know their titles and have a few scraps of quotations. Whether *Prometheus Bound* was the first play or the second, it was followed by one called *Prometheus Unbound*, in which Heracles kills the eagle and releases the Titan. Ancient commentators suggest that Prometheus revealed his secret – that the son of Thetis will be stronger than his father – just before Zeus was about to mate with her; she was safely married off to a mortal named Peleus, and their son, of course, turned out to be Achilles. Shelley found this conclusion dismaying, and he had no interest in simply reconstructing the lost play. He writes in his Preface, 'I was averse from a catastrophe so feeble as that of reconciling the Champion with the Oppressor of mankind. The moral interest of the fable which is so powerfully sustained by the sufferings and endurance of Prometheus, would be annihilated if we could conceive of him as unsaying his high language and quailing before his successful and perfidious adversary.' So Shelley set himself a different task: to rewrite the missing play as Aeschylus ought to have written it, with the outcome reversed. He rethought the Prometheus legend in its entirety, retaining Aeschylus' dramatic framework but drawing freely from classical and Christian myth and from the whole of human history up to the French Revolution.

THE ACTION

Shelley begins his play at the same point Aeschylus began, and ended, his, with Prometheus bound to a precipice. It is night and he is alone. In his opening speech he defiantly addresses the distant Jupiter (Shelley uses the Roman name for Zeus) and predicts that the hour will come that will drag the cruel king to Prometheus' feet, 'which then might trample thee / If they disdained not such a prostrate slave. / Disdain? Ah no! I pity thee' (I.51–3). This reconsideration or change of heart from disdain to pity is the moral turning point of the play, and it comes astoundingly early. Though the climax of the play, with its own ironic reversal, is the sudden overthrow of Jupiter in Act III Scene 1, shortly after the midpoint, all the action unfolds from Prometheus' initial change of mind with what in retrospect we can see as irresistible necessity. On first reading the play we may feel a suspenseful interest in what Jupiter might do, how Prometheus will respond to it, whether Asia will accomplish her mission, which side Demogorgon is on, and so on, but there is no real uncertainty over the outcome. It is not stretching the term too much to say that the whole of *Prometheus Unbound* is a denouement, an unknotting or unbinding of the plot that Aeschylus knitted in *Prometheus Bound*, and if it troubles us that the unknotting should come at the beginning of the play we should imagine it as the final play of a trilogy. Perhaps the closest Shakespearean parallel in a single play is *The Tempest*, whose stormy and tragic opening scene quickly yields to a kind of comic purgatory whose paradisal outcome is never in doubt. An even closer though non-dramatic parallel is Dante's *Divine Comedy*, where Dante's turn or conversion in the first canto leads to a divinely guided spiritual purification through hell, purgatory, and heaven.

Prometheus no longer hates (57): 'I am changed so that aught evil wish / Is dead within' (70–1). He now wishes to 'recall' the curse he once breathed on Jupiter (59). Voices from the natural realm recite their memories of the devastating effects of the curse, because it was a fall of nature as well as a fall of humanity. Prometheus demands to 'hear that curse again' (131), but his mother the Earth tells him he cannot understand 'the language of the dead' (138); she recounts how she rejoiced when she heard the curse that made the almighty tyrant grow pale and how mortals still preserve it as 'a treasured spell' (184). When Prometheus insists, Earth tells him to summon a ghost to repeat the curse, and he calls on the Phantasm of Jupiter. Ione and Panthea, who are Oceanids and sisters of the beloved but absent Asia, begin their role as chorus, commenting on the awful shape that now appears. The Phantasm, as commanded, repeats the curse, in which Prometheus defied Jupiter to do his worst 'on me and mine': 'I curse thee! let a sufferer's curse / Clasp thee, his torturer, like remorse, / Till thine Infinity shall be / A robe of envenomed agony' (286–9). On hearing the curse, Prometheus says, 'It doth repent me . . . I wish no living thing to suffer pain' (303–5). He thus completes his change of heart.

The Earth laments, convinced that Prometheus has been defeated. Mercury immediately arrives, just as Hermes arrived in *Prometheus Bound* immediately after hearing the prediction of Zeus's downfall, and he brings the Furies with him. He demands to know the 'secret' (371) and urges Prometheus to kneel in supplication, but Prometheus will not submit, and cannot even try to (395); Mercury threatens him and tempts him to no avail, and admits he feels pity and remorse. Prometheus replies, 'Pity the self-despising slaves of Heaven, / Not me, within whose mind sits peace serene' (429–30). The Furies then go to work. They represent spiritual or psychological torments, 'shapeless' until the 'shade' of 'our victim's destined agony' invests them (470–72), and they know their victim. They show Prometheus three scenes: man consumed in a feverish pursuit of knowledge, Prometheus' own gift; the gentle Christ, 'Smiling on the sanguine earth; / His words outlived him, like swift poison / Withering up truth, peace and pity' at the hands of the established churches; and 'a disenchanted nation', France, briefly a 'band of linked brothers', all too soon a land where 'kindred murder kin' (542–77). Prometheus groans at the sights, but worse is in store. A Fury reports the human condition today, where 'Hypocrisy and custom make their minds / The fanes of many a worship, now outworn', those who have one virtue lack the others, 'And all best things are thus confused to ill' (618–31). Prometheus replies, 'Thy words are like a cloud of winged snakes; / And yet, I pity those they torture not' – those who are numb to humankind's sufferings. The astonished Fury exclaims, 'Thou pitiest them? I speak no more!' and vanishes (632–4).

His new-found pity remains intact against the worst Jupiter can inflict. Indeed it emerges that what is at stake in this new and more furious contest is less Prometheus' 'secret' than his pity; at least Jupiter's need to know the secret has grown desperate now that pity has replaced hatred and scorn in Prometheus' heart. For pity seems to undermine the very basis of Jupiter's existence, and he will vanish just as abruptly as the Furies did if the factors that sustain him – hypocrisy, custom, hatred, fear, and contempt – are withdrawn. For his part Prometheus grows stronger in endurance and repeats his hope, or faith, that the 'hour' will arrive (644). Earth now offers to cheer Prometheus by summoning the Spirits of human thought as an answer to the Furies; where the Furies revealed the past and present, the Spirits 'bear the prophecy / Which begins and ends in thee!' (690–91). Six of them speak individually, the first four representing rebellion against tyranny, generous self-sacrifice, wisdom of the past, and visionary poetry, while the last two report the struggle between love and desolation or despair. As a chorus they sing of spring's arrival after winter, and how the growth of wisdom, justice, love, and peace is a spring zephyr. And then they, too, vanish, but leave behind, as Panthea says, a kind of musical resonance in the soul. Prometheus feels that these Spirits of hope are all vain but love (808), and he turns his thoughts to Asia, now far away in an Indian vale. Dawn has come, and Panthea departs to find her.

Prometheus is absent from Act II, which is entirely given to Asia's mission on his behalf. In Scene 1 she is alone, expecting her sister to arrive at dawn. Meanwhile she hails the arrival of spring, 'like a spirit, like a thought ... As suddenly / Thou comest as the memory of a dream' (II.1.2–8). Panthea arrives, bearing 'the delight of a remembered dream' (36), which is also 'the music that I bear / Of thy most wordless converse' (52), as if she is simply the medium of love between Asia and Prometheus. Panthea reports her dream: Prometheus appeared transfigured by the shadow of love, his presence flowed into hers, and she heard Asia's name. Asia then 'reads the dream' in Panthea's eyes, and sees Prometheus smiling with the hope 'that we shall meet again' (124). A second dream, which Panthea had forgotten, now appears and cries, 'Follow!' She recalls that she dreamt of early blossoms scattered by the north wind, each stamped with the words 'O follow, follow!' (133–41). Asia remembers a similar dream. Echoes cry out, 'follow'. Follow where? The Echoes sing: 'In the world unknown / Sleeps a voice unspoken; / By thy step alone / Can its rest be broken, / Child of Ocean!' (190–94). They mean Demogorgon. And where is he? Asia must go 'To the rents, and gulphs and chasms, / Where the Earth reposed from spasms / On the day when He and thou / Parted – to commingle now' (202–5), as if to heal the wounds that the original separation of love from Prometheus inflicted on the Earth. The journey will be a descent into a volcano.

Scene 2 is a brief interlude set in a forest through which Asia and Panthea have passed. A chorus of Spirits sings of the forest's sights and sounds, including the Echoes 'which draw, / By Demogorgon's mighty law / With melting rapture or sweet awe, / All spirits on that secret way, / ... to the fatal mountain' (II.2.41–63). Then two Fauns discuss the Spirits, and speculate on where they come from. Asia and Panthea re-appear in the next brief scene among the mountains in the realm of Demogorgon. A portal like a volcano's hurls up 'oracular vapour' (II.3.4) like that at Delphi, and a great change seems to be in the offing. Asia sees and hears the spring thaw unbinding the snow and thinks of Prometheus:

> Hark! the rushing snow!
> The sun-awakened avalanche! whose mass,
> Thrice sifted by the storm, had gathered there
> Flake after flake, in Heaven-defying minds
> As thought by thought is piled, till some great truth
> Is loosened, and the nations echo round
> Shaken to their roots: as do the mountains now.
>
> (36–42)

In 'Mont Blanc' the river and ravine were analogues of the mind and its experience, while the mountain itself transcended human metaphors. Here the mountain resembles the bravest human minds, who defy superstition while thinking ever more loftily. There the ineffable Power was enthroned on high, here 'the remotest Throne' is 'In the depth of the Deep, / Down, down!' as the spirits sing (61–82). If it is only a false power that occupies heaven, one must seek the true power deep within the earth.

Scene 4 is set in the cave of Demogorgon, who is 'a mighty Darkness / ... Ungazed upon and shapeless' (II.4.2–5). In a sort of reverse catechism, he instructs Asia by answering her questions in cryptic brevity, as if to draw out from her what she already knows in her own depths. Indeed the descent to Demogorgon is in part a descent into her own soul. He answers 'God' to her first few questions, perhaps to suggest that 'Who made X?' deserves no better reply. 'I spoke but as ye speak', he explains later (112). One of her demands is surprising, if Asia is really the embodiment of love set free by Prometheus' retraction of his curse: 'Utter his name – a world pining in pain / Asks but his name; curses shall drag him down' (29–30). That vengeful demand is perhaps a sign that, if Prometheus needs to reunite with love, Asia needs to reunite with wisdom, and that her dialogue in the depths is her preparation for the reunion. Demogorgon's refusal to utter the name prevents her from repeating Prometheus' error. In any case, she then recites the long story of the genealogy of the gods. Under the reign of Saturn humans were happy but fainted for lack of wisdom. 'Then Prometheus / Gave wisdom, which is strength', not to mortals, as we would expect from the established myths, but 'to Juplter' (43–4). That seems to be Prometheus' first disastrous error, more fundamental than the curse, for soon famine, toil, disease, and war fell upon the human race. Seeing their plight, Prometheus sent them hope, love, fire, speech, song, and all the arts and sciences. Now, 'while / Man looks on his creation like a God / And sees that it is glorious', someone or something 'drives him on, / The wreck of his own will, the scorn of Earth' (101–3). It cannot be Jupiter, she reasons, for 'he trembled like a slave'

71

when Prometheus cursed him (108). Demogorgon suggests that Jupiter is a slave to evil, but he still will not declare who or·what the master is (if it is not evil itself), for 'the deep truth is imageless'. We might already have guessed that it is Prometheus, but Demogorgon hints that it is 'Fate, Time, Occasion, Chance, and Change', or some principle underlying these, embodied perhaps in Demogorgon himself. Yet he then adds, 'To these / All things are subject but eternal Love' (116–20), implying that Asia herself is at least their equal if not their superior. She asks one last question: When shall Prometheus arise? The answer: Now! Cars or chariots appear, one for each Hour. A charioteer with a dreadful face is the Hour of Jupiter's eclipse, another with 'dovelike eyes of hope' (160) is the Hour of Prometheus' release, and it will carry Asia and Panthea just behind the first.

As they ride in their chariot (Scene 5), Asia is radiant with a dazzling beauty. Panthea tells of Asia's birth, and we see that she is a version of Aphrodite (Venus), goddess of love and desire. Spirits sing praises to Asia, 'Life of Life' and 'Lamp of Earth' (II.5.48, 66), while she replies that her soul is 'an enchanted Boat' (72) floating on the music. Like the mysterious boat that rides upstream in *Alastor*, she and Panthea have passed the realms of Age, Manhood, Youth, and Infancy, in that order, 'Through Death and Birth to a diviner day' (103), and Asia envisages the 'Paradise of vaulted bowers' (104) that will be hers when she rejoins Prometheus.

The climax of the drama is the overthrow of Jupiter in Act III Scene 1. It is interesting that Jupiter makes his only appearance in the scene of his disappearance, as if to suggest that to see him clearly is to see through him. Also appearing for the only time is Thetis: she never speaks, but Jupiter quotes her anguished speech when he raped her, relishing the memory of his male pride, his 'penetrating presence' (III.1.39). Like a good dramatic climax Jupiter's overthrow comes at the moment he expects his power to be consolidated, for 'henceforth I am omnipotent' (3). He concedes that 'The soul of man, like unextinguished fire,' – Prometheus' gift – 'Yet burns towards Heaven with fierce reproach and doubt / And lamentation and reluctant prayer, / Hurling up insurrection' (5–8), but now that Prometheus has withdrawn his curse Jupiter has no fears.

> Even now I have begotten a strange wonder,
> That fatal Child, the terror of the Earth,
> Who awaits but till the destined Hour arrive,
> Bearing from Demogorgon's vacant throne
> The dreadful might of ever living limbs
> Which clothed that awful spirit unbeheld –
> To redescend and trample out the spark [.]
> (18–24)

The ironies here are complex. Jupiter seems already to have learned the traditional (Aeschylean) secret of Prometheus and to have felt undissuaded by it. He believes his fatal child is 'Mightier than either' of its parents, as he tells Thetis a moment later (44). So it becomes clear that the secret known to Prometheus 'Which may transfer the sceptre of wide Heaven' (I.373) has less to do with a possible child of Thetis than with 'the destined Hour' (III.1.2.) of the transfer, that is that such a transfer is destined. Jupiter thinks his son will act as a kind of Black Prince at his father's behest, snuffing out the last hopes of humanity. Indeed he seems to think his son has already overthrown Demogorgon himself, leaving his throne vacant and expropriating his might. Of course, what Jupiter says here is truer than he knows, for Demogorgon has left his throne and is about to arrive in place of the son. Is there a son? He believes Thetis conceived one, but we never hear her story: perhaps the son is Jupiter's 'conception' only, or 'misconception'. The salient echo of Milton's account of the 'begetting' of the Son by God – 'This day I have begot whom I declare / My only Son' (*PL* V.603–4) – seconds the implication that the son does not exist, for Shelley thought the doctrine that Jesus of Nazareth is the Son of God to be mere imposture. His long note on Christianity in *Queen Mab*, in fact, is attached to a speech of God's that echoes Milton's: 'I will beget a son, and he shall bear / The sins of all the world' (VII.135–6).

Are we to understand, then, that Jupiter's child is really Demogorgon? He is not the son of Thetis, but he tells Jupiter, 'I am thy child, as thou wert Saturn's child, / Mightier than thee' (III.1.54–5). Perhaps that means that he is Jupiter's child only in so far as he is mightier than the current ruler and will overthrow him. Yet it is true that sooner or later tyranny breeds its own overthrow, and it is very much in the Aeschylean mode of imagery to call such an overthrow its child. 'For it is the impious act,' the Chorus of the *Agamemnon* sings, 'that begets many more after it, resembling their parent' (758–60). Perhaps, too, Shelley is implying that tyranny is really sterile. It can only smother life, not create it, and tyranny's attempts to consolidate itself are chimerical and self-defeating. Whatever the allegorical meaning, Jupiter's summoning of his phantasmal 'son' is parallel to Prometheus' conjuring of the Phantasm of Jupiter: Prometheus recalls the curse and thereby reveals the real Jupiter to be no more than a phantasm, while Jupiter learns that his existence rested on nothing more solid than a misconception. With that, Demogorgon embraces him, and both fall 'down – ever, forever, down' into the 'bottomless void' (81, 76).

Scene 2, set on the island of Atlantis, is an interlude like Scene 2 of Act II, where minor characters discuss the doings of major characters. Ocean, an ineffectual comforter and mediator in *Prometheus Bound*, here speaks

73

with Apollo, regent of the sky and sun. When Apollo reports Jupiter's fall, Ocean resolves that the sea will turn calm, navigable, and even musical, and Apollo rejoices that he will no longer gaze down on sorrowful deeds. Apollo hears the music of dawn, and departs to perform his daily task.

The great reunion takes place in Scene 3, which begins with Hercules, in a cameo appearance, unbinding Prometheus and declaring (in three and a half lines) that strength serves wisdom, courage, and love. The very brevity of Hercules' part, presumably a long one in the lost original play, bespeaks the negligible role of violence in a true revolution. Prometheus then announces to Asia and her sisters that they and he will withdraw to a beautiful cave 'Where we will sit and talk of time and change / As the world ebbs and flows, ourselves unchanged' (III.3.23–4). Their roles in the renovation of the world are completed, and they will live on in a transcendent realm of thought and art. He asks Ione to give a 'mystic shell' (71) to the Spirit of the Hour, through which he is to trumpet the good news to the world, and then return to the cave: time will stop for the loving community, it will be perpetual spring. He then turns to Mother Earth, but before he can speak she reports a deep transformation of her plants, animals, and people, a restoration of the Garden of Eden. She describes their new life 'in happy dreams' and their new death in a peaceful return to Earth (95–107). Asia is troubled at the notion that living things can die, and the Earth tells her what she told Prometheus in Act I: that as an immortal he cannot understand the language of the dead. She reminds us, too, implicitly, that no human beings, with the possible exception of Hercules, ever appear on stage. All the characters are immortal beings, even Jupiter, who is now at the bottom of nothingness but, as we infer at the very end of the play, might return if the human race fails again in its spiritual power.

Earth goes on to describe a cavern, presumably the same one Prometheus knows, and gives it to the lovers. Finally she summons a Spirit rather like Eros or Cupid, whom she calls 'my torch-bearer' (148), and enjoins him to conduct them to a temple that used to bear Prometheus' name, where 'emulous youths' carried 'The lamp which was thine emblem' (168–70). That alludes to the Athenian festival of the Lampedophoria ('Lamp-Bearing)', the instituting of which probably concluded the final play of the original trilogy (whether *Prometheus the Fire-Bearer* or *Prometheus Unbound*). Beside the temple is the cave.

The forest before the cave is the setting of Scene 4. The Spirit of the Earth steals the scene with his childlike teasing, but he reports seriously enough the transformation that came over the inhabitants of a city he passed *en route*, apparently, to the temple and cave. He had seen 'Hard-featured men, or with proud, angry looks / Or cold, staid gait, or false and hollow smiles / Or the dull sneer of self-loved ignorance / Or other such foul masks' (III.4.41–4). Then there was a loud but sweet sound, from the shell of the Spirit of the Hour, 'and soon / Those ugly human shapes and visages / . . . / Past floating through the air . . . / . . . and those / From whom they past seemed mild and lovely forms / After some foul disguise had fallen' (64–70); even toads and snakes grew beautiful. In a moment the Spirit of the Hour returns, and his report of the great transformation expands on that of the Spirit of the Earth. It is largely in negatives, but among the most eloquent negatives Shelley ever wrote.

> None frowned, none trembled, none with eager fear
> Gazed on another's eye of cold command
> Until the subject of a tyrant's will
> Became, worse fate, the abject of his own
> Which spurred him, like an outspent horse, to death.
> None wrought his lips in truth-entangling lines
> Which smiled the lie his tongue disdained to speak;
> None with firm sneer trod out in his own heart
> The sparks of love and hope, till there remained
> Those bitter ashes, a soul self-consumed,
> And the wretch crept, a vampire among men,
> Infecting all with his own hideous ill.
>
> . . .
>
> The loathsome mask has fallen, the man remains
> Sceptreless, free, uncircumscribed – but man:
> Equal, unclassed, tribeless and nationless,
> Exempt from awe, worship, degree, – the King
> Over himself; just, gentle, wise – but man:
> Passionless? no – yet free from guilt or pain
> Which were, for his will made, or suffered them,
> Nor yet exempt, though ruling them like slaves,
> From chance and death and mutability,
> The clogs of that which else might oversoar
> The loftiest star of unascended Heaven
> Pinnacled dim in the intense inane.
>
> (137–48, 193–204)

With this stirring speech Act III ends, and, as we might gather from the sense of rhetorical closure, it ends the play as Shelley conceived it in April 1819. It was a three-act version that he sent to his publisher, essentially as we have it but lacking a few short lyrical passages that he inserted later in the year. The play feels rounded and complete. There are no loose ends in the plot, and even the afterthought about passions in the very last lines does not disturb us much. (In fact, in the ending of the later Act IV, there is a similar afterthought, and a rather more disturbing one.) Yet Shelley decided to add another act, and what he wrote is the most sustained lyrical outburst in all his work.

Act IV is more a pageant or masque than an act in a drama. No more drama, in fact, is possible, for its field of action, historical or linear time, has ceased. Jupiter, the 'King of Hours', is now a corpse (IV.20), the 'past Hours' have vanished (31), and the new Hours have no chariots (56) - they no longer race but walk or dance. The chorus of Hours sings: 'Once the hungry Hours were hounds / Which chased the Day, like a bleeding deer / ... But now - oh weave the mystic measure / Of music and dance and shapes of light' (73–8). The Hours are joined by 'the Spirits of the human mind' (81), whom we last met as they consoled Prometheus in Act I, and they all dance and sing together. Panthea and Ione serve as commentators on this display and on those that follow, and some of their speeches are in blank verse. All the rest are in one or another lyrical measure, with lines of varying lengths and meters and intricate rhyme schemes.

Let us look at one unobtrusive example, ten short lines (30–39) passed between Ione and Panthea.

> IONE
> What dark forms were they?
>
> PANTHEA
> The past Hours weak and grey
> With the spoil, which their toil
>   Raked together
> From the conquest but One could foil.
>
> IONE
> Have they past?
>
> PANTHEA
>   They have past;
> They outspeeded the blast;
> While 'tis said, they are fled
>
> IONE
> Whither, oh whither?
>
> PANTHEA
> To the dark, to the past, to the dead.

It may be difficult for many readers today to appreciate the beauty of such a passage, but it might help to think of it as the text of a duet set to music. Shelley was quite interested in opera and ballet, and there is reason to think that his subtitle to the play, *A Lyrical Drama in Four Acts*, is meant to invoke musical forms of theatre. He knew, too, that ancient Greek choral parts were originally sung and danced; the texts that survive are feeble one-dimensional transcripts which, as Shakespeare's Theseus says, our imaginations must amend. Since Shelley was not a composer, and did not expect his play to be performed with or without music, he could only try to create the effects of music through rhythm and rhyme in spoken verse. At this, I think, he was supremely skilful.

The end-rhyme scheme divides this passage into equal halves, each opening with a question from Ione: *aabcb / ddece*. We might look at each half as two couplets, but with the second couplet in each half parted by one line of another couplet (*c*) which thereby links the halves, as if the rhymed couplets are dancing couples, pairing and parting and pairing again with other mates. The middle line of each half is really two rhyming half-lines, so the scheme becomes *aabbcb / ddeece*. The first line of the second half, moreover, is split in a manner the Greeks called *antilabe*, though the Greeks did not use rhyme; here the *d*-rhyme word 'past' is repeated. The very shortness of the lines embodies their subject, the fleetingness of the past Hours, with perhaps a self-reflexive gesture in 'While 'tis said, they are fled', which suggests the fleetingness of speech as well. But speech is arrested in its flight by the musical form of its saying, and indeed it is the passing of these Hours that inaugurates the choral dance of eternity. So this little form 'answers' Ione's questions by incorporating them, as it were, into a dense dance of rhymes.

Time is transfigured into tempo. The section begins with parallel lines with three stresses in a row, 'What dark forms' answered by 'past Hours weak', after which an anapaestic pattern prevails, as if the slow crawling hours of the past deserved one last rhythmical salute before the lighter and faster Hours of the new day take over. The fourth and ninth lines, the *c*-rhymes, are not anapaests but adonics, named for Sappho's lament for Adonis, the dying and reborn god: 'raked together' (assuming two syllables in 'raked') echoed in 'Whither, oh whither?' This last of Ione's three questions is answered in the last and longest line, in three anapaests, 'To the dark, to the past, to the dead', which beautifully picks up 'dark' from Ione's first line and 'past' from three earlier occurrences before sealing the whole ten-line duet with the finality of 'dead'.

This sort of artistry is apparent everywhere in Act IV, but the overall effect of the act is that of a spontaneous outburst of spiritual energy.

Many readers have disliked it, and have borrowed the last words of Act III, 'intense inane', to describe it. It is Shelley at his most idealistic, in his most sustained attempt to embody his utopian vision, his sense of what it might feel like to arrive at a realm of complete social and imaginative freedom. It draws from ancient traditions such as the music of the spheres, transformed as we might expect into the music of the earth, as well as from Dante's spectacular sound-and-light display in his *Paradiso*. Astounding things are seen and heard.

Panthea and Ione see two visions floating on music (202–3), the Spirit of the Moon and of the Earth, each elaborately and mysteriously described as infants within their respective spheres. In the Earth's sphere Panthea sees 'the melancholy ruins / Of cancellea cycles' (288–9), the remains of former civilizations overwhelmed by a flood, along with ancient animal forms, as if they were annihilated by a God in a passing comet who undid the work of the Creator by a negative fiat: 'Be not.' The Earth, in other words, is reborn; old Mother Earth has become, in spirit, her own child. The burden of the past is shrugged off. Not only the cycles of the past but also cyclicity itself is cancelled, for we are no longer caught in the interminable tit for tat of injury and revenge, of vengeful furies inflicting new vengeance-provoking crimes; instead, we have entered a new world of love and forgiveness. Shelley has, in a way, reversed the cycle of the Christian year, which passes from Advent and the Nativity through Lent and Easter: he takes us instead from the scene of crucifixion, Prometheus impaled on the rock, to the birth of a godlike child.

There are in fact two godlike children, a male Earth and female Moon, and they now sing their duet. The 'boundless, overflowing bursting gladness' of the Earth (320) penetrates the 'frozen frame' of the Moon (328) as he celebrates tyranny's annihilation and love's fulfilment (350–55). This is Eros on a cosmic scale: love makes the world go round, and makes the moon go round the world. The love that transforms humans, even as a leprous child is healed by spring waters, also governs the universe the way the sun rules the maze of planets (388–99). The Moon, 'thy chrystal paramour' (463), tells how she revolves about the Earth as the Earth speeds around the Sun: 'I, a most enamoured maiden / ... / Maniac-like around thee move, / Gazing, an insatiate bride, / On thy form from every side' (457–72). Though Shelley knew all about Newton and the laws of gravity, he reverts to the ancient doctrine that the force of 'attraction' that unites all things is a kind of love, a form of the same force that unites men and women and infuses all life.

At this point, surprisingly, Demogorgon reappears. As Asia summoned him to action in Act II, so the song of love between Earth and Moon, particularly the Moon's 'chrystal accents [which] pierce / The caverns' of Earth (499–500), seems to prompt him back on stage. He addresses in turn the Earth, the Moon, the heavens, the elements, all living things, all meteorological forces, and man, and when he has their attention he gives the final speech of the play. He recapitulates in a few words the defeat of despotism by love, and praises 'Gentleness, Virtue, Wisdom and Endurance'. He then intrudes a relatively realistic note: the possibility that this eternal spring might not last eternally. 'And if, with infirm hand, Eternity, / Mother of many acts and hours, should free / The serpent that would clasp her with his length' – alluding to the brief final release of Satan in the Book of Revelation – 'These are the spells' – Gentleness, Virtue, and so on – 'by which to reassume / An empire o'er the disentangled Doom' (562–9). The dispiriting thought arises that we might have to do this all over again: 'To suffer woes which Hope thinks infinite; / To forgive wrongs darker than Death or Night' (570–71). Yet his point (and he ought to know) is not so much that eternity will inevitably slip back into cyclical time or that man will lapse again into violence and tyranny as that, if these things happen, we will have the means to return to paradise. If Hope thinks the new round of woes is infinite, she will have forgotten the lesson Demogorgon is here to teach. And we, presumably, will have one advantage over past generations of enslaved humanity, a handbook of hope and wisdom called *Prometheus Unbound*.

Levels of Meaning

That, more or less, is the plot of the play, though I have been unable to resist pausing at a few points to quote or comment. Reduced to its barest outline, the plot is a chain of events consequent on the first (and only) act of Prometheus. Prometheus repents and retracts the curse, Panthea flies to Asia, Asia descends to Demogorgon, Demogorgon dethrones Jupiter, Prometheus is freed and united with Asia, they retire to a cave, and the earth and heavens celebrate.

In interesting ways the play observes the three traditional dramatic unities. The unity of time is clear enough. It is night in the Indian Caucasus at the opening of Act I and morning by the end of it (I.813); morning in the vale at the opening of Act II and approaching noon by the end, for the Spirit of the Hour tells Asia and Panthea 'We shall rest from long labours at noon' and 'The sun will not rise until noon' (II.4.173, II.5.10); it is just before dawn in Act III Scene 2 but the setting is much farther west, in the Atlantic; it is presumably noon when Prometheus is released in III.3; and after that there seems to be no time at all. In a sense the whole play takes place in no time at all. Once Prometheus withdraws his curse night yields to day, that is, the long nightmare of history comes to an end, and in that day, or 'Hour', everything happens simultaneously. We might say that Prometheus' change of heart, Asia's quest for Demogorgon, and Demogorgon's annihilation of Jupiter are different aspects of the same deed, different symbolic embodiments of the same truth. That is the classical 'unity of action' in a complex form. We saw in *Alastor* how Shelley reduced a narrative movement to a repetition of similar gestures; in *Prometheus Unbound* he has, rather miraculously, spun out into a long dramatic sequence a single deed.

Though the play does not, on the face of it, observe the unity of place, the play's vast geographical reach, from the Hindu Kush to 'Atlantis', loses significance as the characters flit rapidly from one locale to the next, and shrinks to nothing in the final act, where the Earth and the Moon replace Prometheus and Asia as cosmic lovers.

What kind of play is this? As a genre it is comedy. It even conforms, more or less, to the pattern of classical 'New' Comedy, where a young man outwits the father of a young woman and marries her. Jupiter, who has 'father' (*pater*) in his very name, corresponds to the *senex iratus* or angry old man, found in nearly every comedy from Menander through Shakespeare to Hollywood movies, and Demogorgon corresponds to the clever servant who carries out the crucial trick. Asia resembles many Shakespearian heroines in being more active than the hero. Act IV formally resembles the play-within-a-play in Act V of *A Midsummer Night's Dream*, and even more both the bergamask that concludes that play and the fairy dance that concludes the larger play; it is also a little like the masque Prospero puts on for Ferdinand and Miranda in *The Tempest*. The original Prometheus trilogy, of course, was technically a tragedy, but not all plays performed at the tragic festival were tragic in plot. The only extant trilogy, Aeschylus' *Oresteia*, is composed of two tragedies followed by a comedy that crowns the story with a happy ending, and apparently the *Prometheia* trilogy ended the same way (to Shelley's disgust), in a compromise that settles the dispute. Shelley would also have known that tragic trilogies were usually followed by a fourth play, a farcical satyr play that sometimes mocked the themes that preceded it. He translated one of them, Euripides' *Cyclops*, and his own satire *Swellfoot the Tyrant* owes something to both the satyr play and the comedies of Aristophanes, which Shelley had been reading in 1818. Satyr plays had a chorus of satyrs led by Silenus, whom Shelley's fauns mention at the end of their little scene (II.2.90). Shelley's decision to write a fourth act for *Prometheus Unbound*, then, might have been influenced by his knowing that the Athenians watched four plays in a row during the Festival of Dionysus. Dionysus, too, the patron god of theatre, is mentioned or alluded to several times in Shelley's play.

Rather puzzlingly, Shelley devotes several paragraphs of his Preface to acknowledging and defending his absorption of 'contemporary writings'. To resist the influence of a great contemporary would be 'strained, unnatural, and ineffectual'. A Poet combines internal powers with external influences. 'Every man's mind is in this respect modified by all the objects of nature and art; by every word and every suggestion which he ever admitted to act upon his consciousness; it is the mirror upon which all forms are reflected, and in which they compose one form.' Whatever criticisms Shelley may be warding off here, we might take this last clause as a description of *Prometheus Unbound* itself: a single form that reflects all forms. Tragedy, comedy, and satyr play; monologue, dialogue, and choral ode; blank verse and rhymed forms of every imaginable kind; opera, ballet, and masque – all are subsumed in an epic grandeur. Indeed, besides Shakespeare and the Greek dramatists, the two precedents Shelley singles out in his Preface are Milton and Dante, who wrote the two greatest Christian epics. Dante, whose *Divine Comedy* gives the sense of 'comedy' most appropriate to Shelley's play, is praised for his imagery drawn from 'the operations of the human mind'. In Milton's *Paradise Lost*, the character of Satan is the 'only imaginary being resembling in any degree Prometheus' in that they share 'courage and majesty and firm and patient opposition to omnipotent force' – we can sense Shelley's temptation to shock the pious by adopting the first rebel as his hero – but he will not do for his purposes because Milton gave him many faults as well as virtues. Shelley, then, though he modestly disavows any comparison with these greats, none the less invites it with such citations, and, beyond that, suggests that his play is not only a correction of the first dramatist but a kind of compendium of world literature in both content and form.

In turning now to the larger meaning of the play, we must begin with Shelley's own claim that 'Prometheus is, as it were, the type of the highest perfection of moral and intellectual nature, impelled by the purest and the truest motives to the best and noblest ends.' The word 'type' suggests we are to read the play as an allegory, though the little hesitation in 'as it were,' and the traditional use of 'type' itself, may give us pause. In medieval usage, as we find it in a famous letter attributed to Dante, the 'typological' level of meaning, whereby the events of the Old Testament are read as types or prefigurations of events in the New Testament, is also called the 'allegorical': it turns the allegorical into something historical, the fulfilment or perfection of an incomplete past. With Dante's fourth level of meaning, the 'anagogical', which refers to the final fulfilment or revelation at the end of time, we are also not far from Shelley's play, the timeless last act of which is his own version of the Book of Revelation. But it is the third level, sometimes called the 'moral', that is closest to Shelley's definition of Prometheus: it is the dimension that calls on us here and now to change our lives. Is Shelley offering Prometheus as a role model? He goes on to say that he is presenting 'beautiful idealisms of moral excellence', but can types and idealisms be human enough for us to emulate?

Interpreters of the play have not agreed on just what allegorical formula best defines Prometheus. It is clear that Prometheus is not a mortal human being, for he is a Titan and immortal, and that he does not stand for anything mortal within the human soul, for he cannot even understand the language of mortals (I.138). Yet he is certainly in some way human. If he is the type of the 'highest perfection of moral and intellectual nature', then his transcendence of mortality suggests that there is some aspect of the human psyche that is perfectable and therefore immortal. The fact that Prometheus retires to a cave where he will sit with Asia and her sisters and talk of time and change, 'As the world ebbs and flows, ourselves unchanged' (III.3.23–4), near a temple that preserves Praxitelean sculpture as in a museum (III.3.161–6), suggests that Prometheus somehow contains humanity the way form holds content, or the way speech is 'about' a topic. The forms of art and science, the highest creations of the human mind – these gifts of Prometheus are eternal, and serve as constant beacons to direct our imperfect souls onward and upward. Prometheus might then be taken as the highest consciousness of which the human mind is capable, a condition in which we are, in some sense, immortal. Shelley did not believe in personal immortality, and detested the Christian belief in rewards and punishments in the afterlife, but he entertained the ancient idea that an impersonal part of us, the intellect, may return to the 'One', or *Nous*, which he called the 'One mind', after we die. Life is a dream, a bad one, and when we die (perhaps) we will awaken to an expanded state of being, where we will comprise an indistinguishable part, without any personal consciousness, of the whole. The part that will survive might be called the Promethean.

The most influential modern interpreter of the play, Earl Wasserman, defines Prometheus as the One Mind, as absolute existence as constituted by thought; Prometheus is not an allegorical abstraction from human minds so much as the source and ground of mind from which individual human minds are abstracted. This is itself a very abstract idea, and it is not clear how convincingly it can be derived solely from the text of the play; not all scholars agree. Some have taken Prometheus as one of the faculties of the human mind, like one of the four psychic components or 'Zoas' into which

William Blake breaks up his character Albion, the universal man. Prometheus might then stand for the imagination, or even the poetic faculty, which created the human world but then lapsed into the condition in which we see him in Act I, a dependence on the rocky natural world and its overlord, both of which the imagination has forgotten it invented in the first place. To recover the truly human world, a world of loving 'intertranspicuous' relationships (IV.246), requires less an act of will than an act of imagination, an act that recalls or recollects the powers projected on to the 'external' world and taken as real.

Whether he is the One Mind or the imagination or something else – and it will be wise when reading the play not to let any formula reduce one's openness to its richness – the most interesting question is Prometheus' relationship to Jupiter. As Asia tells the story to Demogorgon, 'Prometheus / Gave wisdom, which is strength, to Jupiter' (II.4.43–4), who must have existed before his tyranny over Prometheus; it is a little hard to square this passage with the otherwise compelling thesis that Jupiter is a product of Prometheus' erroneous mind. Perhaps Asia does not have the story right, as she is still seeking wisdom from Demogorgon, or perhaps Asia only dimly understands the truth, that Prometheus projected his own wisdom, mistakenly, out from himself and in so doing created Jupiter. Jupiter clearly stands for 'God', among other things, whose origin in human error Shelley described in *Laon and Cythna*:

> What then is God? Some moon-struck sophist stood
> Watching the shade from his own soul upthrown
> Fill Heaven and darken Earth, and in such mood
> The Form he saw and worshipped was his own,
> His likeness in the world's vast mirror shown [.]
>
> (3244–8)

The form becomes an object of faith and fear, and then a curse on the human race. To represent Prometheus' curse as the Phantasm of Jupiter is a brilliant stroke, for the 'real' Jupiter is no less a phantasm dreamed 'up' by mortals, who then compound their error and greatly complicate their return to sanity by cursing their own creature. Prometheus' 'secret' then, is not only the certainty that the hour of Jupiter's overthrow is coming, as we claimed earlier, but the knowledge that his overthrow lies entirely within our power: we need only undo what we once did. It is as much a memory of the past as a prophecy of the future.

If Jupiter stands for a division of the human consciousness, the exiled Asia seems to stand for another division. Jupiter, perhaps, gained his tyrannical power in two stages, first through the epistemological error of taking an upthrown shade for an independent reality, and then through the moral error of cursing it when it seems to curse us. Asia, then, as a separate being, would be a product of the second error: the exile of love from the psyche. Hesiod gave Prometheus no wife; in Aeschylus' play the chorus once refers to Prometheus' wife Hesione, an Oceanid; it is in Herodotus that we find his wife named Asia, another Oceanid. Choosing the name Asia may have been part of Shelley's 'orienting' of the play farther east than Aeschylus sets it. The original play is set in Scythia, somewhere in the remote north or northwest of Greece, though other traditions place Prometheus in the European Caucasus mountains. Shelley moves him to the Indian Caucasus, or Hindu Kush, through which the Poet of *Alastor* wandered in search of the origin of things. Shelley knew the tradition that it was the birthplace of the human race; what we call the Caucasian race would be a later development in the European Caucasus. The reunion of Asia and Prometheus, then, might signify the reunion of the far-flung human race.

It is also, however, a reunion of the male and female portions of the human psyche, a return to the androgynous state that ancient philosophers speculated was our original unfallen condition. By making Prometheus' beloved into a personification of love itself like Venus, of course, Shelley is taking the male point of view: Prometheus is the subject of love, Asia the object of love. Asia is rather like Beatrice, who represents divine love to Dante, and the 'Eternal Feminine', who draws Goethe's Faust ever onward. Shelley makes up for the male-centredness of his allegory, however, by making Asia the hero of an epic quest. Like Dante and Faust, like Gilgamesh and Odysseus and Aeneas and many other (male) epic heroes, it is Asia who undertakes the journey to the monster in the deep, a descent to Hades where she learns the past and the future, while Prometheus is still bound to his rock. Shelley did something similar in *Laon and Cythna*: though the older Laon has taught Cythna her revolutionary ideals, it is she who organizes the revolution through her eloquence while Laon is recovering from his torture. She even rescues him on horseback!

Demogorgon is the most baffling of the four major figures. His name is not found in any ancient literature, though Lucan describes a nameless 'superior' god who dwells in an underworld beneath the underworld. The name seems to have arisen in the middle ages through a blunder by a scribe, who miscopied the Greek word *demiourgos* into *demigorgos* or something similar. The *demiourgos* or 'demiurge' is the creator of the world in Plato's *Timaeus*. Once *gorgos* got accidentally inserted into the name, it seemed to refer to the Gorgons or the most famous Gorgon, Medusa. The syllable *demi* or *demo*, which means 'people', then seemed odd, so sometimes it was respelled as 'daemogorgon', as if it were a cross between daemon (or demon) and gorgon. Boccaccio, Spenser, and Milton all name him: he has become a sovereign power dwelling beneath the earth, inferior only to the Christian God. Peacock refers to 'Arcadian Daemagorgon' in his poem *Rhododaphne* (1818) and appends a learned note. That Demogorgon was worshipped in Arcadia, though never by name, as Peacock says, may motivate the scene with the fauns (II.2), which has an implicitly Arcadian setting. Three of Shelley's sources have a witch or goddess who descends to consult or command Demogorgon; they are thus precedents for Asia. That he dwells beneath a volcano makes Demogorgon kin to the Titan Typhon, who Aeschylus' Prometheus predicts will erupt out of Mount Etna, where he has been confined by Zeus.

It may or may not be significant that Prometheus, the one mind or highest faculty of the mind, never comes into direct contact with Demogorgon. Does that suggest that he is unknowable, some force beyond perception or even comprehension? Love sets him going but cannot see him on his throne. Asia's dialogue with him, as we have noticed, is something like a dialogue with her own heart (II.4.121). When Jupiter asks who he is, Demogorgon replies, 'Eternity – demand no direr name' (III.1.52), but that is no more definitive than his cryptic answers to Asia. We might take a stab at it by saying he stands for the inherent actuating force of the universe, the 'Power' of 'Mont Blanc' or the 'Spirit of Nature! all-sufficing Power, / Necessity!' of *Queen Mab* (VI.197–8). He might be called latency or potentiality, the ever-imminent power that humans can activate or actualize when they summon sufficient wisdom, imagination, and love. To personify such a tenuous concept may seem superfluous and even self-defeating, since 'the deep truth' that Demogorgon represents is 'imageless', as he says (II.4.116). The prospect of showing Asia overthrowing Jupiter by herself may have convinced Shelley that he needed an intermediary figure, and the symbolic implications grew a little murky. Shelley, however, as we might expect of an admirer of Dante, constructed several further allegorical levels, one of which, the social or political, may have required this fourth and most shadowy of figures.

Jupiter is King as well as God, or rather he is the principle of tyranny in society as well as in morality and religion. Just as God is a misconception or false product of human minds, so Monarchy is a fallen state of society, a misconstruction out of our collective weakness. Shelley seemed to agree with those Enlightenment philosophers who argued that the people, taken as a whole, get the government they deserve: if they cannot maintain the virtues necessary for an egalitarian republic, then tyranny and oppression will arise in their midst. Rousseau, Paine, and Godwin, among others, made this case, and even the older Coleridge, who had abandoned his youthful republicanism, wrote in 1822 a sentence that might have been a commentary on *Prometheus Unbound*: 'A Tyrant is only a monstrous Phantasm up-streaming from the grave and corruption of the huddled corpses of the self-murdered Virtue and inner freedom of the People, *i.e.*, the Majority of the Citizens of the State.'

Prometheus, in this view, would represent the intellectual forces of resistance, the philosophers and poets and virtuous citizens who refuse to sacrifice their intellects on the altar of despotism. The retraction of the curse and the simultaneous liberation of love would represent a national resolution to heal the divisions of society and no longer to cherish, as the Earth does in Act I, the memory of ancient quarrels, however nobly fought. That Prometheus is unable to remember his curse (I.137, 302) suggests he has already arrived at the point society must attain if it is to break the iron chain of injury and retaliation: the granting of amnesty. To forgive is to forget; amnesty is amnesia. One of the paradoxes of the play is that the 'recall' of the curse, its recollection or *anamnesis* (Plato's term), is also its 'recall' in the sense of retraction. We must remember what we have forgotten, that we brought about our own enslavement, in order to forget what we remember, the hatred that sealed that enslavement.

Asia, then, is the love that replaces that hatred. Her flight in a chariot just behind the Hour of Demogorgon is a way of saying that brotherhood must immediately follow the overthrow of tyranny. The French Revolution is the great example of how not to do it, in Shelley's view, for despite the noble rhetoric of fraternity it turned within three or four years to terror and new tyranny, first under Robespierre and then under Napoleon. The usual excuse for this failure was that the long ages of monarchy and religious superstition rendered the French people unfit for the rational and tolerant behaviour that alone can sustain liberty, equality, and fraternity. 'The French were in the lowest state of human degradation,' Shelley wrote in *Proposals for an Association of Philanthropists* (1812), 'and when the truth, unaccustomed to their ears, that they were men and equals was promulgated, they were the first to vent their indignation on the monopolizers of the earth, because they were the most glaringly defrauded of the immunities of nature.' He repeated the point in his *Philosophical View of Reform* (1819–20): 'the oppressed, having been rendered brutal, ignorant, servile, and bloody by long slavery, having had the intellectual thirst excited in them by the progress of civilization, satiated from fountains of literature poisoned by the spirit and the form of monarchy, arose and took a dreadful revenge on their oppressors.' Right after the Furies show Prometheus the bloody degeneration of the French Revolution, 'a low yet dreadful groan / Quite unsuppressed is tearing up the heart / Of the good Titan' (I.578–80), but he endures the agony, and looks ahead to the revolution of a later day, where love will be at work from the beginning.

Demogorgon, in this political framework, might stand for 'the people'. Shelley chose to spell the name, not as Peacock had it (Daemagorgon or Daemogorgon) but as Milton did, and brought out the etymology of the first half, 'people'. Demogorgon might mean 'monster of the people'. Anti-Jacobins such as Edmund Burke had characterized 'the mob' as 'a swinish multitude', and others had seen the people as a monster such as a hydra. Working-class radicals in England had brought out journals with such ironic titles as *The Gorgon* and *The Medusa*. Volcanoes, too, are ancient symbols of revolutions or uprisings. There are problems, however, with this definition of Demogorgon. Why does he disappear back into the abyss with Jupiter? We would expect him to emerge transfigured, the 'Demos' without the 'Gorgon', after removing the power that saw the people as gorgonian in the first place. (He does reappear for the closing speech of Act IV, but not as the voice of the people.) His plunge with Jupiter sounds violent, both in Jupiter's description of it as 'inextricable fight' (III.2.73) and in Apollo's account of it in the next scene, whereas we would expect Jupiter merely to evaporate, first into a phantasm and then into nothing. We also wonder what is going on between Asia and Demogorgon in his cave. One politically minded critic has suggested that Asia is a kind of political agitator, like Cythna in Shelley's early epic, who instructs and provokes the working-class Demogorgon through a dialogue. This cannot be right, for surely it is he who instructs her. Love, it is true, seems to release the power or potentiality that he symbolizes, but the essential action in this scene is Asia's education, not his. She attains wisdom through love while Prometheus attains love through wisdom; their reunion ratifies the union each has achieved alone. That is all that is needed to annihilate Jupiter, who is the principle of disunion. In embracing Jupiter, Demogorgon imitates the union of Prometheus and Asia; he is the negative pole of the same union. The Phantasm of Jupiter was 'a frail and empty phantom' (I.241) coughed up by a volcano (I.231–32), and now Demogorgon erupts to take Jupiter back where he came from. Demogorgon seems to be a metaphysical category more fundamental than anything political, though it may manifest itself in political events; he is not a class of people but a power or law of events.

We noted in passing that nature goes through the same cycle of ruin and redemption as human beings do and as the chief characters do. If we take Prometheus as the 'One mind' or absolute consciousness, then nature has no existence independent of this mind. Shelley maintained there was no essential difference between 'thoughts' and 'external objects', for the latter are simply 'thoughts which affect a number of persons at regular intervals' (as opposed to irregular thoughts affecting a few persons, such as dreams and hallucinations) (*Treatise on Morals*, uncertain date). On these grounds, the fall of humankind and of nature are the same thing, just as Christians have believed, in an erroneous framework, for a long time. Prometheus asks the mountains, springs, air, and whirlwinds to repeat the curse, for they suffered under it no less than mortals did (I.59–111). This identification of mind and nature accounts for the many naturalistic details, often precisely in keeping with current science, that add up to yet another allegorical level of *Prometheus Unbound*. The 'crawling glaciers' of Prometheus' torment (I.31) become cataracts and avalanches from 'thaw-cloven ravines' when Asia approaches the portal to Demogorgon's volcano (II.3.34). Her description of the volcano itself is based on Shelley's visits to Vesuvius and Avernus near Naples. The two fauns in the previous scene are interested in the bubbles that rise from the bottom of lakes and then burst to release 'fiery air' into meteors that in turn sink under the waters. They are describing the 'hydrogen cycle' whereby methane is released and oxidized, making will-o'-the-wisps. The repressed energies of nature are bubbling up while Asia and Panthea pass overhead.

When Jupiter took power, 'the unseasonable seasons drove, / With alternating shafts of frost and fire,' humans into caves (II.4.52–4; cf. I.268). That may remind us of Milton's account of the tilting of the earth's axis 'twice ten degrees and more' and the resulting extremes of 'pinching cold and scorching heat' (*PL* X.668–706). The cosmic dance of the spheres in Act IV, celebrating the natural order restored on Jupiter's defeat, echoes in turn the 'Mystical dance' of the planets of *Paradise Lost* (V.618–27) (cf. *PU* IV.129–334). Shelley brings in the water cycle, electricity, magnetism, the nebular hypothesis, organic evolution, infra-red radiation, and the synchronic rotation of the moon, among other things, and yet subsumes them all under metaphors of lovers, families, and government. Besides elaborating the identification of mind with its 'objects', this act gives the play an encyclopaedic character, as if it is to be a *summa* of all essential knowledge imaginatively grasped.

Before leaving *Prometheus Unbound* we should take up the subject of 'wordless converse'. That is the phrase Panthea uses when she comes to Asia with the dream-communication from Prometheus: 'I am made the wind / Which fails beneath the music that I bear / Of thy most wordless converse; [I am] dissolved / Into the sense with which love talks' (II.1.50–53). Already in the first act language or speech has been put into question. The Earth tells Prometheus that he will not understand his own curse for it must be uttered in 'the language of the dead': 'Thou art immortal, and this tongue is known / Only to those who die' (I.138, 150–51). His incomprehension is partly explained by his earlier avowal 'that aught evil wish / Is dead within' (70–71). The language of the dead, we might guess, concerns itself only with dead wishes and other mortal subjects. The Earth knows the other language but 'I dare not speak like life, lest Heaven's fell King / Should hear' (140–41). She then mentions 'the inarticulate people of the dead', as if they have no language at all, though they cherish the curse (183–4), and she goes on to say that the only way for Prometheus to hear the curse is for him to summon a 'ghost' from the world of death where images of the living, including Prometheus himself, may be found. When Jupiter's Phantasm rises, he asks, 'What unaccustomed sounds / Are hovering on my lips, unlike the voice / With which our pallid race hold ghastly talk / In darkness?' (242–5). Presumably it is the language of the living that the Phantasm speaks, or rather 'A spirit seizes me, and speaks within' (254), as if he were the priestess at Delphi in the grip of Apollo. This is all a little confusing. There is nothing like it in Aeschylus or Hesiod, though Shelley may have been developing Homer's idea that there is a language of the gods and a language of mortals. Shelley's point seems to be that the curse, once living but now declared dead within Prometheus, must be displayed as dead or 'officially pronounced dead' through a final utterance by a ghost, a ghost whose own tenuous existence depends on the memory of the curse.

Prometheus has learned his lesson, we can see, when he later refuses to say the name of Jesus Christ: 'Thy name I will not speak, / It hath become a curse' (603–4). After seeing the images the Furies unveiled, he asks Panthea to spare him the woe of speaking what he beheld (646–7). After four of the human Spirits sing their news, Panthea loses her voice, though Ione finds hers (758–9). Though Panthea has a great deal to say to Asia in the next scene – as she must, in a drama meant to be read – she ostensibly communicates her dream-vision of Prometheus' transfiguration directly through her eyes. 'Lift up thine eyes,' Asia says, 'And let me read thy dream' (II.1.55–6). Panthea then gives a long speech, presumably for our benefit, but Asia claims 'thy words / Are as the air. I feel them not . . . oh, lift / Thine eyes that I may read his written soul!' (108–10). Eyes are the traditional inlets of love and outlets of soul, and Asia has no trouble seeing Prometheus within Panthea's. A picture is worth more than a thousand words: direct visual intuition or vision is a 'wordless converse' of a different order from speech, whether living or dead. If a readable 'written soul' must be written in some language or other, it is none the less a language of a radically different kind. We seem then to have three kinds of language so far: the language of the dead, the language of the living, and the visionary 'language' of the soul and of love.

The truths these modes of language convey are all either statable or picturable, unless the inarticulate dead can grasp no truths at all. Shelley may be adapting the scholastic distinction between discursive reason, which human beings have, and intuitive reason, which God and the angels have. In any case, Demogorgon says 'the deep truth is imageless' (II.4.116), implying there is yet another kind of language that transcends vision as well as words. Asia understands him, for her heart has anticipated his answer, 'and of such truths / Each to itself must be the oracle' (122–3).

Shelley has set himself an impossible representational problem. He is writing a play, a closet drama that will only be read, silently or aloud, so he can only resort to words even when he wants to assert their inadequacy. He can paint word pictures, like Panthea's speech to Asia, but they are not the real thing. He compounds his difficulty by positing a deep imageless truth and a deep imageless character who embodies that truth. Demogorgon may be 'a mighty Darkness' (2) and 'Ungazed upon and shapeless' (5), but he nevertheless has a name, can speak and act, and is 'described' by various characters, not always negatively.

One way out for Shelley is through the illusion of simultaneity or instantaneousness I discussed earlier. If, after reading the play several times, we can hold it in our minds as a complex object revealed all at once from many viewpoints, we will have acquired something of the intuitive or visionary power that Shelley claims will one day be a universal gift. Another solution is to turn to an intuitive form that language can convey, at least in part: music. Melody and harmony may have no strict counterpart in language, but poetry shares rhythm or metre, timbre or tone-colour, and certain formal structures like the sonata or theme and variation. Rhyme is a little like a chord and much like a repeat or echo. We saw in *Queen Mab* and elsewhere how often Shelley invokes music as accompaniment to his highest visions and as an analogy for many of the deepest processes of the mind. Beginning at the end of Act I of *Prometheus Unbound* music becomes an ever more insistent theme. Asia hears the 'Aeolian music' of Panthea (II.1.26), who describes herself as the wind failing beneath the music she bears from Prometheus. His voice, she reports, 'fell / Like music' and lingered 'Like footsteps of far melody' (65–6, 88–9). Asia's dream concludes in music shaken by wind from the boughs of trees (156–7), and that same music emerges out of her dream as the Echoes sing in 'liquid responses' a 'wild and sweet' song (171, 185) that draws Asia and Panthea towards the mountain. The fauns in the next scene are struck by the way the nightingales pass their song on from bird to bird:

when one, 'sick with sweet love, droops dying away', another will 'catch the languid close' and lift 'The wings of the weak melody' (II.2.24–40), just as Panthea passed her melody to Asia. At the end of their scene the fauns depart in the hope of hearing 'those wise and lovely songs' (91) of old Silenus, one of which, the unbinding of Prometheus, will charm to silence even the nightingales.

Without multiplying details we can sum up: music enters the drama quietly as a simile at the end of Act I (I.802–03) and then as a 'weak melody' early in Act II, but then seems to widen and deepen in the middle acts. In the final scene of Act III we hear the report of 'a sound, so loud, it shook / The towers amid the moonlight, yet more sweet / Than any voice but thine [Asia's], sweetest of all, / A long long sound, as it would never end' (III.4.54–7). That music marks the great transformation of the human race. The culmination and triumph of music is one of the subjects of the final act, and it is no less the form of the act itself. Except for the descriptive speeches of Ione and Panthea in blank verse, its language is entirely lyrical, entirely raised to the condition of music. Indeed, as the Spirit of the Earth sings, 'Language is a perpetual Orphic song, / Which rules with Dædal harmony a throng / Of thoughts and forms, which else senseless and shapeless were' (IV.415–17). Language rules thought the way Orpheus ruled the beasts through his music, but more than that, language at its highest is music itself. Panthea rises 'as from a bath of sparkling water, / A bath of azure light, among dark rocks, / Out of the stream of sound' (503–5): the river of life in which we are baptized to rise transfigured is the river of music. Panthea is an emblem of us, Shelley's intended readers, as we allow the music of his 'lyrical drama' to flow over us.

Music, then, is the wordless language of love. It is also the language of hope, and it is on hope, even more than on love, that Demogorgon dwells in his final speech. It is for us 'to hope, till Hope creates / From its own wreck the thing it contemplates' (573–4), and it is certainly to encourage our hopes in the face of general moral ruin and despondency that Shelley wrote *Prometheus Unbound*. In doing so he has transformed his primary literary sources in yet another way. In Hesiod's *Works and Days*, Zeus sends the woman Pandora as the price men must pay for Prometheus' gift of fire. Pandora opens her jar and every evil flies out to torment the human race, while Hope alone remains trapped inside it. That would seem to suggest that Hope does not dwell among men, which is obviously untrue now, and that Hope is an evil like all the other contents of the jar, which is debatable. Perhaps Hesiod imagined that Hope, a good thing, was preserved in the jar as a treasure to help the mortal race endure the evils that escaped. Shelley might have read the story as saying that Hope was withheld from mortals by a vengeful Zeus. That would suit the passage in Aeschylus' play (250–53) where Prometheus tells the chorus that, besides fire and many crafts, he gave mortals 'blind hopes', in defiance of Zeus, in order to make mortals stop foreseeing their death. Aeschylus' meaning may be that only if they forget they are going to die can mortals live with any happiness, but Shelley may have seen in it the idea that mortals should stop worrying about death, which, for all we know, is only a gateway to a higher impersonal life. Byron was wrong to say that we can foresee only our wretchedness and resistance. Shelley would have disagreed with Aeschylus, too, that hopes are blind, for the Hope that he celebrates throughout his play is visionary. Hope, in fact, is almost synonymous with Prometheus' 'secret'. So long as humans cherish the hope that tyranny will fall and love will govern the world then they have not been utterly defeated. And if they have not been utterly defeated, they will inevitably prevail.

6 'Ode to the West Wind'

Shelley sometimes describes poetry as an object or force that appeals to our intellect. 'It awakens and enlarges the mind itself,' he writes in the *Defence*, 'by rendering it the receptacle of a thousand unapprehended combinations of thought. Poetry lifts the veil from the hidden beauty of the world'. Its appeal to our emotions arises through its intellectual or visionary effect. Even love, the 'great secret of morals' that poetry nurtures, Shelley describes not as a passion but as an empathy or 'a going out of our own nature, and an identification of ourselves with the beautiful' found outside ourselves. Yet sometimes Shelley describes poetry as a vehicle of feelings, pleasure, and enthusiasm, as we noted near the end of the discussion of 'Mont Blanc'. Most of Shelley's own poems are filled with vehement feelings, ecstatic, mournful, passionate, desperate, or fiercely indignant, and many of them turn inward to talk about himself.

Perhaps as a way to resolve these conflicts – between a serene, almost classical ideal of poetry and a more romantic and affective one, between selflessness and self – Shelley often combines an artful mastery of form with what seems a cry of his heart. In no poem is this combining of contraries sharper than in 'Ode to the West Wind', one of his two or three best-known poems. It is a violent plea to the wind to seize him, to fill him with itself, as if it were a prayer by an ecstatic maenad to be rapt or transported by Dionysus, and it is 'composed' in a strict and intricate stanzaic pattern. A line that many readers have found embarrassingly self-pitying – 'I fall upon the thorns of life! I bleed!' (54) – is tied inextricably by rhyme, image, and theme to the rest of the poem. Such a contrast to some extent belongs to the tradition of the Greek ode: we find it as early as the 'Ode to Aphrodite' by Sappho, written in the demanding stanza named after her, and the choral odes to Dionysus in Euripides' *The Bacchae*. Shelley goes much farther than the ode form requires, however, and makes his ode a *tour de force* about uncontrollable force itself.

In October 1819 Percy, Mary, Claire, and the rest of the household moved to Florence, where they stayed about four months. There a son was born, the only one to outlive childhood, named Percy Florence. The city, which had been the centre of the Renaissance, the 'foster-nurse of man's abandoned glory, / Since Athens, its great mother. sunk in splendour' (*Marenghi*), was glorious still, at least in its artistic and natural beauty.

93

despite the sunken state of Italian politics. Shelley spent many days studying the painting and sculpture of the Uffizi Gallery, and he probably reread Sismondi's *The Rise of the Italian Republics*, which praised republican Florence as the new Athens, the shining home of individual liberty and great art after the long medieval night. Early in his essay *A Philosophical View of Reform*, which he was writing during his months in Florence, Shelley credits the city's resistance to Empire and Popedom with 'the undisputed superiority of Italy in literature and the arts over all its contemporary nations' and 'that union of energy and of beauty which distinguishes from all other poets the writings of Dante'. A 'union of energy and beauty' would well describe the contrasting features of Shelley's Ode, too. More important, this passage reminds us that as he wandered about the city he was inescapably in the presence of Dante, its greatest poet.

Not that Dante wrote anything remotely like 'Ode to the West Wind' – except perhaps the final canto of the *Paradiso* with its prayer 'that I may leave to the people of the future one gleam of the glory that is Yours' (XXXIII.70–72). It is that Dante, like Shelley, was an exile from his birthplace and, like Shelley, wrote about it and for it, in verse and prose, out of prophetic anger and love. 'Dante was the first religious reformer,' Shelley wrote later in the *Defence*, and, as Sismondi also claimed, he was the first modern citizen-poet, more passionate about the renovation of his country than the salvation of his soul. We shall consider later to what extent Dante is somehow figured in the poem, but at the outset we can see in the very form of the Ode that Shelley is paying him tribute.

Each stanza of the Ode is made of fourteen lines of *terza rima*, the form Dante made his own in *The Divine Comedy*, with the rhyme scheme *aba bcb cdc*, and so on. In Dante the three-line stanzas or tercets run on at great length, forty or fifty to a canto, and resolve themselves . . . *wxw xyx yzyz* at the end. For every rhyme but the first and last, then, there are three instances, or as Dante might say, three hypostases, suggesting the three persons of the Trinity; they also reflect the triptych structure of the whole poem and the thirty-three cantos in each third (plus one as introduction). The inner rhyme of one tercet exfoliates or flowers as the outer rhyme of the next, or as Wasserman describes it in a metaphor drawn from the Ode, on the death of one tercet the seed in its grave gives birth to the flower of the next. Shelley's stanzas are brief, however, and he resolves them differently: *aba bcb cdc ded ee*. There are four tercets and a couplet, with five rhymes, which anticipate the five stanzas of the whole; the final couplet at the end is unlike Dante but much like a Shakespearean sonnet. And indeed by giving each stanza fourteen lines Shelley invented the *terza rimá* sonnet, a merging of the forms of the two greatest modern poets. (There were a few *terza rima* odes in English before Shelley, which he probably did not know, but no *terza rima* sonnet. A century later, one of Shelley's greatest admirers, Robert Frost, wrote one called 'Acquainted with the Night', much more Dantean in tone and theme than those of the Ode.)

The argument of the Ode is divided in the proportion of three to two: the first three stanzas are rhetorically similar, each directly addressing the west wind and calling on it to 'hear!' in the final line, and the last two stanzas turn inward to the speaker and then outward again in a final plea. Key words, images, and ideas echo and interweave as if they were also rhymes (leaves are in each stanza, for example), though something fresh and unpredictable continually emerges. Some readers have been puzzled at this virtuoso craftsmanship lavished on what purports to be an uncontrolled outburst provoked by an uncontrollable natural force. In 'Mont Blanc' Shelley used a highly irregular 'form' for the supposedly spontaneous meditation occasioned by another transcendent natural Power. He had before him recent odes by Wordsworth and Coleridge that varied with every stanza. The regular stanzas of 'Hymn to Intellectual Beauty' are a closer precedent, but for this Ode he invented a very strict form with apparently no kinship to the content. He ends by asking that his words be scattered among mankind, and it seems he wanted them to be wrapped in the most beautiful and permanent package: since what is at stake is his power as a poet, he wanted to prove he had not lost it. Both these motives may have coalesced in his tribute to a great Florentine predecessor whose poetic power had gloriously proven itself in the face of exile and the censorship of the church. For out of a seed planted during a single terrifying night of loss and during a dawn of renewed hope, blossomed the most formally perfect and intellectually exacting poem of the modern world.

To directly address a natural object is to animate it, to breathe human consciousness or soul into it from one's own lips: direct address is the essential poetic act. 'O wild West Wind, thou breath of Autumn's being': the wind is the breath-soul or spirit (like Latin *spiritus*, akin to *spirare*, to breathe; or Greek *psyche*, akin to *psychein*, to breathe, blow). It comes into existence in the poem in the first breath of the poet, who also animates the season by giving it a breath; he is preparing for the breath that the west wind of the spring will need to blow her clarion. It is the inspiration, the 'breathing in' of the 'Wild Spirit', that he needs at the outset of a poem, an invocation to the Muse before an epic. Here, of course, the entire poem is the invocation, and the epic is only implicit, perhaps, as the future poetry and prophecy he hopes to be strong enough to write.

> O wild West Wind, thou breath of Autumn's being,
> Thou, from whose unseen presence the leaves dead
> Are driven, like ghosts from an enchanter fleeing,
>
> Yellow, and black, and pale, and hectic red,
> Pestilence-stricken multitudes . . .
>
> (1–4)

The restless anthropomorphizing energy here is, well, breath-taking. The wind is called a breath, and we expect something about its blowing away the leaves, but 'breath' is immediately withdrawn (for the moment) and instead the leaves are 'driven' by an unnamed agent (Death?) before the invisible presence of the wind. In a little lesson in poetry-writing, Shelley breathes life into the dead metaphor of 'dead leaves' by inverting the words, not just for the rhyme but to make us see that the leaves really are dead, and therefore resemble ghosts. By the third line we are in a third metaphor, where the wind is an enchanter or conjuror, and we cannot help thinking that we the readers are being driven about rather like leaves, by a poet who conjures up metaphors at will. We may wonder, too, that the leaves, which are the visible and even colourful manifestations of the invisible wind's power, should be likened to ghosts, which are usually invisible, while the unseen wind should be compared to a presumably flesh-and-blood enchanter. And why are they fleeing rather than gathering round the conjuror? The onward rush of the syntax (we do not have a sentence yet) does not allow time for much wondering, however, though we might notice that 'enchanter' has 'chant' in it, a song or a poem or a 'Dirge' (23), something done with the breath. Perhaps the enchanter has pronounced a pestilence on the leaves, though plagues are traditionally wind-borne anyway. The leaves are 'multitudes', as if they are people. Are the four colours the four races of humankind? Or four diseases, corresponding to the four humours? Or the four elements, which will play a part in the structure of the poem? We are left in any case with the first vivid visual image in the poem, before Shelley takes another breath and recasts the metaphor.

> O Thou,
> Who chariotest to their dark wintry bed
>
> The winged seeds, where they lie cold and low,
> Each like a corpse within its grave, until
> Thine azure sister of the Spring shall blow
>
> Her clarion o'er the dreaming earth, and fill

(Driving sweet buds like flocks to feed in air)
With living hues and odours plain and hill:

Wild Spirit, which art moving everywhere;
Destroyer and Preserver; hear, O hear!

(5–14)

The triplets of the verse seems to inspire three kindred images, each showing a phase of the tree's life-cycle in its appropriate season. First the leaves are forcibly 'driven' by or before the autumn wind, then the autumn wind more gently drives (in a chariot) the seeds to their beds where they sleep for the winter and only seem to be dead, and finally we see the spring wind like a careful shepherdess 'driving' the buds in the air. There are also three similes: the leaves are 'like ghosts', the seeds are 'Each like a corpse', and the buds are 'like flocks'. Since there are only two winds, however, the first and third images mirror each other more fully, rather like the *aba* pattern of each tercet. The 'azure' spring wind answers the 'unseen' autumn wind, her clarion answers his implicit chant, and the 'living hues' of the buds answer the four colours of the dead leaves. This intricate set of correspondences reflects the unquestioned assumption in this stanza that, at least as far as trees are concerned, spring will come. We get both major phases, dying and rebirth, in equal weight, with the phase between them confined to a dream. The inevitability of the natural cycle seems to be bodied forth in the structure of this stanza. Since Shelley will end the poem with a question precisely about this inevitability, we notice here something of the traditional gesture of the pastoral elegy, which he will repeat in *Adonais*: nature renews itself every spring, but the one we mourn will not come back. Perhaps the flocks in parenthesis are meant to suggest this traditional genre, though we understand that here it is the elegist himself who has fallen and may die.

If stanza one is about earth, with graves, plain, and hill, stanza two is set in the air, in the 'steep sky', while stanza three is set on the sea, or under it, for the wind is 'moving everywhere'. The fourth element, fire, appears as lightning in stanza two but as a distinctly human spark only at the end.

Thou on whose stream, 'mid the steep sky's commotion,
Loose clouds like Earth's decaying leaves are shed,
Shook from the tangled boughs of Heaven and Ocean,

Angels of rain and lightning: there are spread
On the blue surface of thine aery surge,
Like the bright hair uplifted from the head

> Of some fierce Mænad, even from the dim verge
> Of the horizon to the zenith's height,
> The locks of the approaching storm.

$$(15\text{--}23)$$

Just as each tercet of *terza rima* contains two rhymes that tie it to the preceding tercet and one that ties it to the following, so this stanza about events in the air looks back to the preceding stanza with 'Earth's decaying leaves' and forward to the next with 'Ocean' and especially with the 'stream' of air and the 'aery surge'. Clouds resemble leaves, air resembles water; air and water, which jointly produce clouds, must then resemble trees whose boughs, entangled by the storm, shake off their leaves. With all these tangled resemblances, it is no wonder that these lines have led some influential critics to fault Shelley for having a poor grasp of visual or concrete things. Just what is it we are supposed to be seeing? Some have cited references in Shelley's essays or letters to the water spouts that sometimes come with autumn storms off the Italian coast. Products of air and water themselves, the spouts somewhat resemble trees, though whether they have tangled boughs is doubtful, and whether they look like tangled boughs themselves, as the image demands, is even more doubtful. One should not underestimate Shelley's capacity for exact observation, but to seek exact observation here may not be to the purpose. It is the 'commotion' here, not the objects, which Shelley is mainly concerned to embody in metaphors, the shedding and shaking of leaf and cloud and not the leaf and cloud themselves, or at least not the other things connected with leaf and cloud in the natural world. In the similes of Homer, whom no one ever accused of lacking a grasp of concrete things, it is often impossible to find a one-to-one correspondence between details; here, after establishing the basic correspondence, it is as if Shelley found an 'unrhymable' term (the shaking bough) in his system, where

shed or shaken leaf : loose cloud :: shaking bough : x.

Since x has to refer to some action of heaven and ocean, Shelley braves out the logic of the imagery: heaven and ocean must each have boughs, and they are tangled. That there is an assertion of poetic wilfulness here we must concede. To use a simile ourselves, just as the west wind, that unseen enchanter, permeates earth, heaven, and ocean with his transforming force, so Shelley, striving with the wind (51–2), permeates his poem with 'forced' metaphors. In any case, if we cannot swallow 'tangled boughs', we would have choked on the invisible enchanter terrifying colourful ghosts in the first stanza.

The point, perhaps, is that the wind is everywhere, and it does the same kind of thing everywhere. It destroys the dead and it preserves the living. What is terrifying about it is that we are not sure whether we are numbered among the quick or the dead.

The second image, about the Mænad, in part restates the first. The clouds that are 'angels' or harbingers of rain and lightning are 'locks of the approaching storm'. Brought to life here is the metaphor buried in the term 'cirrus' for the kind of clouds these are, which is Latin for 'lock' or 'curl'. It is as if Shelley decides here to follow out the logic of someone else's metaphor: if these clouds are a kind of hair, then whose hair is it? And so the fierce Mænad enters, who strictly corresponds to the storm, blown here by the west wind (we must imagine a wind behind her blowing her hair forward even as she races towards us), though she also seems to be one more personification, like the enchanter and his shepherdess sister. She is more like the leaves and clouds, however, for she is driven by the god Dionysus, destroyer and preserver.

According to some legends, Dionysus was a dying and reborn god, a type of the year-god, like Adonis, who is the subject of the first Greek pastoral elegies, which are dirges to the dead. Thus:

> Thou dirge

> Of the dying year, to which this closing night
> Will be the dome of a vast sepulchre,
> Vaulted with all thy congregated might

> Of vapours, from whose solid atmosphere
> Black rain and fire and hail will burst: O hear!

(23–8)

The pagan imagery of Mænads and dying years shifts to Christian or at least gothic provenance – another reminder of fascination with charnel horrors – with a vaulted sepulchre and a 'congrega-tion' of clouds. We seem at once indoors, in a church, and outdoors, exposed to the elements. It seems not only the end of the day and the end of the year but the end of the world, a day of doom as if from the Revelation. But it is the dirge that motivates this image. It is unclear in the grammar whether we are to imagine the year singing a vaguely through the wind or whether the year is simply the subject of Shelley's it, but in either case the wind *is* the dirge; it chants or is requiem mass, complete with the *Dies Irae* or Day of Wrath.

It is interesting that every time Shelley uses the word 'dirge' he associates it with wind: 'The rising tempest sung a funeral rude wind is singing / The dirge of the music dead'; and so on. In *Alastor* he connects them both with hair, as in the Ode: 'his scattered hair / Sered by the autumn of strange suffering / Sung dirges in the wind' (248–50). Three times 'Dirge' appears in a title – 'Autumn: A Dirge' (1820), 'Dirge for the Year' (1821), and simply 'A Dirge' (1822) – and all three times the poem so titled has not only a wind but other features of the Ode. 'Dirge' must have had very distinct private connotations for Shelley, and if one wished to consider his collected works as evidence for how his mind worked (which is not the approach we are taking in this book) these recurrent clusters of associations would be a good place to begin. For the present purpose it is enough to see how the Ode itself is a dirge, sung in counterpoint to the dirge of the wind.

The third realm subject to the ruling west wind is the sea, both the Mediterranean and the Atlantic, and both the surface and the vegetation beneath.

> Thou who didst waken from his summer dreams
> The blue Mediterranean, where he lay
> Lulled by the coil of his chrystalline streams,
>
> Beside a pumice isle in Baiæ's bay,
> And saw in sleep old palaces and towers
> Quivering within the wave's intenser day,
>
> All overgrown with azure moss and flowers
> So sweet, the sense faints picturing them!
>
> (29–36)

ring wind will awaken the earth from its winter dreams (9– n wind has awakened the Mediterranean Sea, blue and filled moss as if still under the spring wind's enchantment. Shelley personifies the Sea and localizes him in a place rather far from a bay off the Bay of Naples near Baiæ, a resort town where the emperors kept villas. Shelley had been there the previous Decem- king at the overgrown ruins at the water's edge. 'Quivering within ve's intenser day' probably means that the palaces and towers are d in a shimmering light reflected from the waves, though it might n that they are reflected on the waves, and there is perhaps a suggestion t they are submerged, as indeed in part they were. In any case, Shelley is noticed that the palaces and towers, or at least the quivering daylight, nly exist when the sea is asleep. Once roiled by the wind the sea will not reflect the sun or the ruins, and once the clouds arrive there will be no sunlight for the sea to reflect.

Virgil mentions Baiæ once in a simile for a huge falling warrior: along the coast of Baiæ a massive stone pile built into the sea collapses and turns the sea into turmoil (*Aeneid* IX.710–16). Perhaps the sleeping Sea is dreaming of emperors' palaces tottering and falling into his waters, though now all is peaceful, before the autumn wind comes. Some readers have found allusions to Shelley's hopes for political change in Italy, for the collapse of kings and kingdoms; in fact the following year Naples proclaimed a liberal constitution and Shelley celebrated it in his 'Ode to Naples'. If the wind is blowing political change in Italy, then the Sea's dreams may be prophetic, just as Shelley longs to be a prophet at the end of the Ode, or the Sea may be entranced by the ancient tyrannies still dominating Italy. Certainly Shelley's hopes for social and political revolution are very much at work in the Ode, but it seems a bit forced to inject them here on the strength of the ruins. It does not seem far-fetched, however, to think of the *ubi sunt* theme: Where are the mighty rulers of yesterday? Fallen and half-forgotten, like Ozymandias, before the irresistible Power of time and change.

The somnolent summer yields to the restless autumn as the scene shifts to the Atlantic.

> Thou
>
> For whose path the Atlantic's level powers
>
> Cleave themselves into chasms, while far below
> The sea-blooms and the oozy woods which wear
> The sapless foliage of the ocean, know
>
> Thy voice, and suddenly grow grey with fear,
> And tremble and despoil themselves: O hear!
>
> (36–42)

We move not only to the Atlantic, where its smooth surface has turned into deep wave-troughs, but under it, where we find woods and foliage just as we found them on the land and (metaphorically) in the air. Just as the trees shed their leaves upon the arrival of the wind in the first two stanzas, the submarine flowers and trees despoil themselves of foliage upon hearing the wind's voice. Shelley's note says that it is 'well known to naturalists' that sea vegetation 'sympathizes' with land vegetation in the change of seasons 'and is consequently influenced by the winds which announce it'. Several naturalists I have asked have denied this phenomenon, but it is the notion of sympathy that is most interesting here whether the defoliation occurs or not. If the plants act in sympathy with their kindred on land, then they are less passive than those 'driven' subjects of the masterful

101

wind; they would be almost human, capable of that going out of one's own nature that Shelley calls love. Perhaps to imply just that, Shelley makes not only the underwater plants but the 'powers' of the ocean itself active participants in their own response to the wind. The powers 'cleave themselves' and the blooms and woods 'despoil themselves', as if they had a choice in the matter. This shift from the passive to the reflexive may prepare for the shift from the natural world, which has been the sole subject of the first three stanzas, to the human world, to the speaker and 'mankind', which is the main subject of the last two. It implies, perhaps, that the poet must learn to make himself passive like the leaves, to cease striving with the wind and let its force somehow do its work in him. He must acquire a natural 'sympathy'. The personifications of natural forces in the opening are answered by a kind of naturalization of human forces in the closing.

The first three stanzas have the same rhetorical structure, and nearly the same syntax. If we were to diagram their syntax, we would draw a large set of branching subordinate clauses down the left side of our paper and nothing on the right except the verb 'hear'. Except for the first line and lines 13 and 14, which frame the first stanza, each of the six apparent sentences, two to a stanza, begins 'Thou' or 'O thou' and then yields its forward momentum to a relative clause governed by 'who' or 'which' or 'whose', all of which modify 'thou'. They amount to huge nouns, composed of adjectival clauses revolving around the pronoun of direct address. They are elaborate names, and as names they repeat the form of the ancient ode, which begins by naming the god and its attributes fully and properly, for if an ode was used in sacred liturgies it would have been of the greatest importance to get all the names and epithets correct. So Sappho begins, 'Throned in splendour, deathless Aphrodite, child of Zeus, snare-braider, I beseech you . . .' There is no precedent, however, for giving over forty lines, and three-fifths of the whole ode, to an attempt to name the god. In Shelley's ode, the very multiplicity of clauses suggests that no liturgical formula could possibly suffice for a god which moves everywhere and brings about such sweeping changes. With each 'thou' the poet makes another attempt to control the 'Uncontrollable' (47), rather like the enchanter whose spells may have failed to keep the leaf-ghosts from fleeing. We saw something similar in the profusion of similes for Intellectual Beauty.

The poet's sustained invocations, however, do make the wind present to us, vividly and in great detail. They are a bravura display of poetic power, and thus a fitting tribute to the power of the wind, who is the god of poetry itself. To 'have striven / As thus with thee' (51–2) is to have emulated the wind, whose continual transformations of land, sky, and sea inspire the poet's continual metaphoric metamorphoses of the wind itself. Perhaps the poet has made himself the passive instrument of the wind, which blows its own horn, as it were, and hears itself through the poet, just as the winds in 'Mont Blanc' come to hear the swinging of the trees they make swing by their coming. At the same time, the repeated plea to 'hear' suggests that the wind is deaf to feeble human prayers, or at least that it is difficult to catch the attention of this great inhuman power; there is certainly something desperate in the tone. To take these two points together, that the poet is proving himself a poet even though the wind may not know or care, we note that 'hear' not only points ahead, to what the poet will say in the following two stanzas, but back, to what has just been said: in effect, 'This is you! Listen! I am a poet!'

Formally, the fourth stanza begins somewhat the way the fourth movement of Beethoven's Ninth Symphony begins, by briefly recapitulating the themes of the first three movements.

> If I were a dead leaf thou mightest bear;
> If I were a swift cloud to fly with thee;
> A wave to pant beneath thy power, and share
>
> The impulse of thy strength, only less free
> Than thou, O Uncontrollable!
>
> (43–7)

It might not have occurred to us that leaf, cloud, and wave were free. That the Atlantic's powers, as we noted, 'cleave themselves' into great waves, in the active voice, may suggest some choice in the matter, but the clouds are 'shed', 'shook', or 'spread', and the leaves are 'driven', all in the passive voice, by the wind. Shelley softens these descriptions here, so that the leaf is borne, not driven, though no less subject to the wind; the cloud seems the equal of the wind, flying 'with thee', not on thee or from thee; and the wave, while 'beneath thy power', passively enough, can also somehow 'share' that power. Trying as usual to do several things at once, Shelley not only shifts the terms towards a free or freer relation with the wind, but suggests a sexual relation between the panting wave and the powerful wind, while preparing for a fourth figure, the poet as a boy. Hence the odd idea that a wave will 'pant': it throbs passionately beneath the wind, it imitates the wind, which is a breath, and it reminds us of the poet himself, who now turns to his boyhood, when he felt at one with the uncontrollable wind.

> If even
> I were as in my boyhood, and could be
>
> The comrade of thy wanderings over Heaven,
> As then, when to outstrip thy skiey speed
> Scarce seemed a vision; I would ne'er have striven
>
> As thus with thee in prayer in my sore need.
>
> (47–52)

We now see that this poem is in part a dirge of a lost boyhood, like such poems of Wordsworth's as the 'Intimations' ode, which Shelley knew well. There is little here of the 'philosophic mind' and calm resignation to the loss of the 'visionary gleam' and 'heaven-born freedom' of childhood, which Shelley incorporated into the last stanza of the 'Hymn'; instead there are striving and prayer. As a boy he had the vision, which scarcely seemed a vision, that he was at one with the wind wherever it blew; now he has lost that vision, he says, and sorely feels its loss. Once, in other words, he felt as unselfconsciously a part of nature as a cloud is, but now feels at strife with it; it was only a vision that he was like the wind, for now he suffers under the burden of the uniquely human awareness of ageing, failed purposes, and death. Though it is his own boyhood that he mourns in the poem, it is interesting to know that Shelley's beloved three-year-old son William had died a few months earlier, the third child to die in their household within a year. Shelley was feeling very old.

> Oh! lift me as a wave, a leaf, a cloud!
> I fall upon the thorns of life! I bleed!
>
> A heavy weight of hours has chained and bowed
> One too like thee: tameless, and swift, and proud.
>
> (53–6)

We wonder at the contradiction here: how can he be both chained and tameless, both bowed and proud? We might have expected 'One once like thee'. The manuscript, however, shows that Shelley considered 'One too like thee, yet mortal – swift & proud', a concession that would avoid the paradox that if he were really 'like thee' he would not have fallen and would not be striving with the wind. Perhaps he decided that 'mortal' is too obvious to need stating, and that he did feel, at the rising of the wind, genuinely tameless, despite the chains. 'One too like thee', moreover, implies that if he were less like the wind he would not feel chained and bowed but would have humbly accepted his woes as most other people seem to do. There is a boast here. Shelley may accept that pride goes before a fall, but he does not accept it as a Christian counsel of humility; to call himself proud in this context is an act of pride, the defiant pride of a Greek hero overcome by tragic circumstances.

Some critics have taken the thorns as an allusion to Christ on the cross, but surely that is to make Shelley's boast more than it is. Nearer to the point, as others have noticed, is Christ's Parable of the Sower, where the word of God is likened to seed sown in various places, which stand for various hearers of the word. 'And that which fell among thorns are they, which, when they have heard, go forth, and are choked with cares and riches and pleasures of this life, and bring no fruit to perfection' (Luke VIII.14). There is an ambiguity in this passage that bears on Shelley's metaphor for himself: while the seed seems to be both the word and the hearers of the word (who in turn seem to be both thorns and victims of thorns, which 'choke' as in VIII.7), Shelley is of course both a leaf and, in the next stanza, a tree that sheds leaves. In fact this allusion prepares us for the conclusion, where Shelley invokes the wind, the 'sower', to send his thoughts abroad like leaves and his words like ashes and sparks. Perhaps there is humility here after all, for Shelley does not liken himself to the 'winged seeds' of the first stanza, though his leaves and sparks serve the same function as the seeds in the Parable.

> Make me thy lyre, even as the forest is:
> What if my leaves are falling like its own!
> The tumult of thy mighty harmonies
>
> Will take from both a deep, autumnal tone,
> Sweet though in sadness. Be thou, Spirit fierce,
> My spirit! Be thou me, impetuous one!
>
> Drive my dead thoughts over the universe
> Like withered leaves to quicken a new birth!
> And, by the incantation of this verse,
>
> Scatter, as from an unextinguished hearth
> Ashes and sparks, my words among mankind!
> Be through my lips to unawakened Earth
>
> The trumpet of a prophecy! O Wind,
> If Winter comes, can Spring be far behind?
>
> (57 70)

Again he begs to become the passive instrument of the god, but again his metaphor, the aeolian lyre, implies that he must himself be in right tune in order to contribute his music, his 'tone', to the mighty harmonies of the wind. He must be actively passive. His relationship to the wind is not unlike that of the 'source of human thought' to the 'everlasting universe of things' at the opening of 'Mont Blanc'. He then immediately compounds the metaphor by bringing in the forest, again much as he did in 'Mont Blanc' (21–4): he and the forest will both contribute a deep, autumnal, dirge-like tone to the wind's music. It may be a little ridiculous to think of the poet losing his leaves as a forest does: just what picture are we meant to imagine? Yet we accept it well enough in Shakespeare's sonnet 73, which of all his sonnets seems most present in the ode:

> That time of year thou mayst in me behold
> When yellow leaves, or none, or few, do hang
> Upon those boughs which shake against the cold,
> Bare ruined choirs where late the sweet birds sang.

Shelley may have also wanted a hint of 'leaves' in its other sense as pages of a book, with an allusion to the 'Sibylline Leaves', those sheets of prophecy scattered by the wind. Of this god of prophecy and poetry Shelley asks to have his leaves of thought and verse published to mankind, to the whole universe; indeed he conjures the wind to do so, 'by the incantation of this verse', punningly echoing the 'enchanter' of the first stanza. As the dead leaves were 'driven' from that enchanter, so Shelley asks this one to 'Drive my dead thoughts . . . Like withered leaves'. Yet here it is he who is the enchanter, not the wind: he has, after all, composed a poem, 'this verse', which not only has a deep autumnal tone but, even more, a tumult of mighty harmonies like the wind itself. The poem has impressively come off, and it seems to register its proud new birth in its own lines.

The logic of the extended tree-and-leaf metaphor dictates that the thoughts that must quicken a new birth are dead, but we may wonder what else is implied here. Surely the thoughts are in some sense alive, like the seeds in the Parable, for even in the parallel image that follows, the words are living sparks as well as dead ashes. Maybe we are to take the leaves as mulch or compost, preparing the ground for a later sower of seeds; this poet then is a prophet in the strict sense, like John the Baptist heralding the saviour in the spring, whose clarion summoned the resurrection of the dead. Yet it is clear that Shelley aspires to be that saviour, to awaken unawakened earth to its mission of social renovation. (For 'earth' as possible hearers, see Jeremiah XXII.29: 'O earth, earth, earth, hear the word of the Lord.') So maybe the thoughts are dead simply because, having been written down, they are the dead letter, as opposed to the living spirit, the 'Spirit fierce' of the wind, in Paul's famous contrast

(2 Corinthians III.6). We might think of them as time capsules, buried to be dug up when the earth is ready to open them, or as the leaflets Shelley launched in miniature hot-air balloons over the Bristol Channel.

We said earlier that the three realms of earth, sky, and sea suggested a fourth term, fire. The image of fallen leaves recapitulates the first stanza, but that of the unextinguished hearth is new, a testimony not only to the poet's unextinguished inventiveness but to his sense that the conclusion, like the final recapitulation of a sonata, ought to contain something new even while harmonizing it with what precedes. It is found also in Shakespeare's sonnet: 'In me thou seest the glowing of such fire / That on the ashes of his [its] youth doth lie'. In his *Defence*, Shelley asserts that even the greatest poet cannot will a poem into existence, 'for the mind in creation is as a fading coal which some invisible influence, like an inconstant wind, awakens to transitory brightness', and 'when composition begins, inspiration is already on the decline'. Awakened by this wind, Shelley hopes now to awaken the sleeping earth, that is, to incite it or inflame it with sparks of his poetry.

For if he has tried to identify himself with the wind in this poem, he also identifies himself with the state of the universe, or at least with Europe in 1819. For the Spring he asks the wind about and longs for in the final lines is not only his own renewal from spiritual death but that of the world from the torpor of tyranny. Indeed they are one. We know that Shelley connected many of his personal sufferings, including his exile in Italy, to the dismal legal and political order of England and post-Napoleonic Europe. He could separate the life of his spirit from the life of his country no more than that earlier exile could whose great poem inspired this ode. Shelley uses the very imagery of the ode to describe him in the *Defence*:

Dante was the first awakener of entranced Europe; he created a language in itself music and persuasion out of a chaos of inharmonious barbarisms ... His very words are instinct with spirit; each is as a spark, a burning atom of inextinguishable thought; and many yet lie covered in the ashes of their birth, and pregnant with a lightning which has yet found no conductor.

Dante passed through a dark winter into spring, and his words still live. Shelley took comfort from his great example and answered the ode's final question with hope.

7   Tyranny and Liberty: Two Sonnets and a Mask

Shelley preferred his tyrants dead. As we saw in *Queen Mab*, *Prometheus Unbound*, and elsewhere, he liked to dwell upon that time in the future when we shall look back on tyranny as dead and on all its great monuments as ruins. That is more than mere resentful day-dreaming, for Shelley saw in all tyrannies an inordinate desire for self-perpetuation, and in all tyrants a lust for eternal fame if not personal immortality. In consigning them all to oblivion, Shelley is striking at what he took to be their ideological heart: if we can so much as imagine them gone and forgotten we have taken a large first step to getting rid of them.

> Where is the fame
> Which the vainglorious mighty of the earth
> Seek to eternize? Oh! the faintest sound
> From time's light footfall, the minutest wave
> That swells the flood of ages, whelms in nothing
> The unsubstantial bubble. Aye! to-day
> Stern is the tyrant's mandate, red the gaze
> That flashes desolation, strong the arm
> That scatters multitudes. To-morrow comes!
> That mandate is a thunder-peal that died
> In ages past; that gaze, a transient flash
> On which the midnight closed, and on that arm
> The worm has made his meal.
> (*Queen Mab* III.138–50)

It is important now, however, while we still have tyrants, to retain just enough memory of past tyrants to remind ourselves from time to time that they are deservedly forgotten, and while that flickering half-life might seem to constitute immortality of a sort it is no comfort to present tyrants to learn that their fame will last only as intermittent moral lessons in future schoolchildren's textbooks. And that is the important function of ruins, most of which were built at a tyrant's mandate.

The most famous of Shelley's sonnets uses a ruin to point his moral.

Ozymandias

I met a traveller from an antique land,
Who said – 'Two vast and trunkless legs of stone
Stand in the desert . . . Near them, on the sand,
Half sunk a shattered visage lies, whose frown,
And wrinkled lip, and sneer of cold command,
Tell that its sculptor well those passions read
Which yet survive, stamped on these lifeless things,
The hand that mocked them, and the heart that fed;
And on the pedestal, these words appear:
My name is Ozymandias, King of Kings,
Look upon my Works, ye Mighty, and despair!
Nothing beside remains. Round the decay
Of that colossal Wreck, boundless and bare
The lone and level sands stretch far away.'

(1818)

To accommodate this subject, unusual for a sonnet, he makes unusual shifts in the sonnet form. There is a syntactic break between octet and sestet but no real turn in the argument or viewpoint, which stays steadily focused on the wreck and its setting; there is no break between quatrains in the octet but a break (but again no turn) between tercets in the sestet. The rhyme scheme has no couplets and no sequence that quite rounds itself out until the end. The *abab* opening is traditional enough, but the *a*-rhyme recurs to lead us into the odd *acdc* pattern. Then the sestet is built of two *terza rima* tercets, *ede fef*, the inner rhyme of the first tercet picking up the stray *d*-rhyme of the octet. That rhyme is the only one that bridges the two parts, and it makes 'things' and 'Kings' stand out a little from the other endings. To pair them is to compare them: kings are lifeless things, it seems to say, even while they are alive.

Ozymandias is the Greek name of the Egyptian pharaoh we know as Ramses II (c. 1304–1237 BC), one of the most powerful of pharaohs, a builder of monuments to himself and a warrior who strengthened the Egyptian empire. 'King of Kings' was a title of diplomatic precision, applicable at that time to the Egyptian and Hittite rulers and perhaps one or two others; lesser rulers were merely 'Kings'. The Greek historian Diodorus Siculus (first century BC) reports the inscription on the statue, which Shelley alters, and he may have had a more recent source, Richard Pococke's *Description of the East* (1743). For all we know Shelley may have met a traveller from Egypt, for his sonnet and his friend Horace Smith's sonnet on the same subject seem to arise from a common conversation but not a common text. In ascribing the report to a traveller from an unnamed land Shelley may lend a slight enchantment to the view, but there is nothing 'romantic' about the character of this absolute tyrant.

The only thing that 'stands' of the once vast empire of Ozymandias is a pair of 'vast' legs that now support nothing. All the rest is broken in fragments half sunk in sand – the sand of the desert that stretches far away but also the 'sands of time' that have flowed for three thousand years. In describing the 'frown, / And wrinkled lip, and sneer of cold command' still extant on the shattered face of Ozymandias, Shelley has taken liberties with Egyptian art, which invariably presented pharaohs with impassive and utterly typical faces. He might have made his point just as well by saying that there is nothing to distinguish this visage from those of a thousand other male Egyptians: all tyrants are alike, and equally forgettable. Instead, Shelley brings out the idea that this broken stone colossus was once connected to a real human being, while naming only those attributes and 'passions' that are in fact utterly typical of tyrants. In doing so he also makes room for the artist, who read his royal subject well.

The syntax of lines 6 to 8 is perplexing until one sees that 'survive' is a transitive verb that takes 'hand' and 'heart' as its objects. The passions are still alive in that, paradoxically, they are stamped on 'lifeless things', the stone fragments of the face. Both the sculptor, whose hand 'mocked' or imitated the passions, and Ozymandias himself, whose heart fed those passions, are long dead. So are the 'works' of the pharaoh, but this work by a nameless sculptor still remains, however fragmented, as both a testament of tyranny's shattered glory and of the sculptor's great skill. If anyone deserves immortality, it is he, not his sneering commander.

The two-line passage carved on the pedestal is wonderfully sardonic. Directed to the other 'mighty' kings of his age, the passage (a command, of course) tells them to despair of rivalling his accomplishments. Directed to the kings of today, it tells them to despair for another reason: let them eclipse even Ozymandias' power, as Britain had already done by 1818, they will come to this in the end, a ruin in the sand. Europe's kings will be lucky if archaeologists dig up a broken statue of them a few centuries hence.

To readers who knew that Ozymandias was Egyptian, an allusion to Napoleon might have hovered over the poem. Napoleon conquered Egypt in 1798, and in 1818, the date of the sonnet, he had been imprisoned on St Helena for three years. This King of Kings had made all Europe tremble, but now 'thou and France are in the dust', as Shelley had written in his sonnet 'On the Fall of Bonaparte' published with *Alastor*. It is also ironic that it was the French invasion that led to the decipherment of hieroglyphics by Champollion, so that, one might fancy, Napoleon could read the inscriptions on the pedestals of the fallen pharaohs. What did he learn?

Britain, in any case, learned nothing, for in 1882 it invaded Egypt and incorporated it into the empire – an empire that would last little longer than the life span of Ozymandias himself.

Perhaps Ozymandias became a doddering fool near the end of his life, and the court eunuchs tyrannized in his name, or his son's name, until the son became god in his turn. Looked at closely, all monarchies are ugly, but at certain phases they are ludicrous and sad. The hereditary monarchical system, Thomas Paine wrote, is 'government through the medium of passions and accidents. It appears under all the various characters of childhood, decrepitude, dotage, a thing at nurse, in leading-strings, or in crutches.' We see that 'the mental characters of successors, in all countries, are below the average of human understanding; that one is a tyrant, another an idiot, a third insane, and some all three together' (*Rights of Man*, Part Two, Chapter 3). By 1819 George III had become all three together, and it is with him, in a memorable opening line, that Shelley begins another sonnet.

England in 1819

An old, mad, blind, despised, and dying King;
Princes, the dregs of their dull race, who flow
Through public scorn, – mud from a muddy spring;
Rulers who neither see nor feel nor know,
But leechlike to their fainting country cling
Till they drop, blind in blood, without a blow.
A people starved and stabbed in th'untilled field;
An army, whom liberticide and prey
Makes as a two-edged sword to all who wield;
Golden and sanguine laws which tempt and slay;
Religion Christless, Godless – a book sealed;
A senate, Time's worst statute, unrepealed –
Are graves from which a glorious Phantom may
Burst, to illumine our tempestuous day.

This sonnet, too, is unusual in form; every sonnet Shelley wrote, in fact, is an experiment in rhyme and structure. The rhyme scheme here – *ababab cdcdccdd* – puts the sestet first, and it has a satisfying structure built around increasingly long syntactic units – one line, two lines, three lines – that play against the regular alternation of rhymes. But there is really no break between sestet and octet. The first twelve lines are a list of items, eight noun phrases (with three or four more included within them) occupying one to three lines apiece; the thirteenth line turns the list into a sentence, equating everything on it with one image, 'Are graves', after which a subordinate clause bursts out with a new thought.

Shelley sent the sonnet to Leigh Hunt to publish, but of course he laid it aside with several other Shelley poems that would only return him to jail if he published them, so it did not illumine our tempestuous day until 1839, when Mary included it in the *Poetical Works*. It is a poem of fierce but controlled indignation. It utters its litany of evils in a tone halfway between a snarling insult and a detached summary of the facts, a balance achieved through the proverb-like concision of the imagery and phrasing. The increasingly assertive *d*-sounds of the startling first line, an improvement on King Lear's self-description as 'A poor, infirm, weak, and despised old man' (III.2.20), reach a crescendo with 'dregs' and 'dull' in the next line before a comic reprise in 'mud' and 'muddy' in the third. The alliterations that follow, 'blind in blood, without a blow', and 'stabbed and starved', are a bit thick, but express very well the scorn of the voice, as if it cannot bring itself to name these vile subjects without striking at them through a kind of harsh verbal magic.

We have seen Shelley's propensity for long skeins of varying images, for an assault by simile, as it were, on whatever ineffable subject draws him (it will reach an extreme in *Epipsychidion*). Here that habit is harnessed to an almost systematic survey of the grievous wrongs of Britain: king, princes, and 'rulers' (mainly aristocrats), in widening categories, then a suffering people, the army, the law, the church, and Parliament. It is quite thorough, and death touches everything and everyone: a dying king, princely dregs, clinging leeches, a fainting country, a people starved and stabbed, liberty murdered, an army that may destroy its commanders, and laws that slay. The whole society is headed for the grave, out of which, possibly ('may'), is to arise 'a glorious Phantom' which, like lightning, will illuminate the storm. This last image, as we shall see shortly, Shelley had just used twice in *The Mask of Anarchy*, first as the mist that rises from the prostrate maiden Hope and becomes a bright inspiring vision (102–25) and then briefly at the end where the slaughter of the people 'Shall steam up like inspiration' (360–63).

Shelley does not indicate just how this resurrection of the dead will take place. If we did not know of Shelley's dismissal of miracles in Christianity, we might take 'Christless, Godless' as implying that a real resurrection of society will be possible only when it returns to Christ and God, who have been neglected by the Church of England, yet perhaps that is finally what it does imply: the Christ we have scorned is the prophet of love and non-violence and the God we have forgotten is the immanent spirit of nature and humanity. The myth of Christ's resurrection is a metaphor for the renewal of the human community even in the face of mass slaughter, whether slow or sudden. This is a kind of Easter sonnet, ending in Hope, and with a kind of apocalyptic expectation born out of the conviction that things could hardly get worse. It is an example of what William Blake called the 'Limit of Opakeness', a consolidation of error, after which a revelation must strike like lightning.

The Mask of Anarchy

The end of the wars with France following Waterloo in 1815 brought new hardship to the majority of the poorer classes of Britain. Returning troops found no work or found it at the expense of others. The removal of the foreign threat also removed the excuse for government repression of the political reform movement, which renewed itself, especially in the northern industrial cities, despite continuing repression. The Corn Law of 1815, which kept the price of domestic grain high by forbidding imports below a certain price, was unpopular with the middle-class factory owners as well as the lower-class labourers. New political journals sprang up, pamphlets such as the radical William Cobbett's 'Address to the Journeymen and Labourers', sold phenomenally (44,000 copies in a month, in Cobbett's case), new organizations were formed, and large rallies were held. In 1819 a series of mass meetings in various cities not only demanded Parliamentary reform and the repeal of the Corn Laws but also elected representatives of their own to a planned national assembly. That was 'sedition', and Lord Sidmouth, the Home Secretary, began pressing county officials to prosecute the leaders and speakers. A Manchester meeting to elect representatives was cancelled, but the following week, on August 16, another meeting was held to petition Parliament for reform.

About 60,000 unarmed and well-ordered workers marched behind their banners into St Peter's Fields. As Henry Hunt, the famous radical orator, began his speech, a squadron of yeoman cavalry began to move towards the platform to arrest him. The crowd blocked the way. A detachment of hussars rode to help the cavalry, both forces slashing their swords about them. The crowd panicked and fled, the horsemen pursued: eleven were killed (including two women), and some four hundred were wounded. Sidmouth wrote a letter congratulating the Manchester authorities, and Baron Eldon, the Lord Chancellor, declared that the meeting had been 'an overt act of treason'. Within a week the affair was dubbed 'Peterloo', in sarcastic praise of a Home Secretary's heroic victory over his own people. A huge outcry spread throughout the country. Hunt was welcomed in London as a hero, new and more radical journals spread, even the London Common Council protested the officially sanctioned violence. In response a fearful government passed the 'Six Acts', which among other things banned large meetings, raised the tax on periodicals, and extended government power in seditious libel cases.

Shelley learned about Peterloo on September 5 in a letter from Peacock, and in hot indignation he wrote *The Mask of Anarchy*, the most passionate, some would say the greatest, of his political poems. It is a long series of irregular but largely tetrameter ballad quatrains (and occasional cinquains) rhyming *aabb* in two couplets. In its simple diction and syntax and its direct address to the common people of England it is Shelley's most serious bid for a popular audience. Hoping that it might have an impact like Cobbett's pamphlet, he sent it to Leigh Hunt, who sat on it as he did the sonnet 'England in 1819' that Shelley sent a little later; it appeared only in 1832, the year of the first great Parliamentary reform, ten years after Shelley's death.

The introductory stanza –

> As I lay asleep in Italy
> There came a voice from over the Sea,
> And with great power it forth led me
> To walk in the visions of Poesy.
>
> (1–4)

– ends with a little letdown, for we might have expected a more heroic response, such as 'To return to fight for liberty.' The remainder of the poem is very strong, but it is weakened at the outset by being pointed out *as* poetry, indeed as 'Poesy'. The opening seems too apologetic for the thunder that follows, but we soon forget it.

> I met Murder on the way –
> He had a mask like Castlereagh –
> Very smooth he looked, yet grim;
> Seven bloodhounds followed him [.]
>
> (5–8)

Right away we see Shelley's strategy: to reverse the procedure of a masque (the title is a pun), where real people wear allegorical costumes. With an effort one might imagine the Viscount Castlereagh, the Foreign Secretary who helped create the system of alliances that ruled Europe after Napoleon, arriving at a real masquerade dressed as a famous murderer; he might have enjoyed the admiration at his daring self-mockery when it came time for the unmasking. He might have counted on his fellow masqueraders' admiration for his bloody reprisals against the Irish after their rising of 1798. But here it is the reverse: Murder wears the mask of Castlereagh. While that reversal allows for a kind of unmasking or exposé – Castlereagh is really a murderer beneath his smooth exterior – he looks so obviously murderous as he tosses human hearts to his bloodhounds (12) that exposure is hardly necessary. The equations are set forth bluntly, as a matter beyond dispute, with no ado about secret truths behind the hypocrisies and ideologies of the ruling order. What is more important is the implication that Castlereagh and all the others are mere masks, mere tools or puppets, of this order; in their march through human history the abstractions Murder, Fraud, Hypocrisy, and so on pick up and drop their willing human slaves with the carelessness with which one might try on or discard a new hat or cravat. Most of them are lesser beings than Ozymandias, and what remains of him? Thus Shelley manages to insult the lordly rulers of Britain as creatures of no account while denouncing their crimes.

Eldon, against whom Shelley had a personal grievance over his decision to deny Shelley custody of his children, Sidmouth of Peterloo, and many more 'Destructions' pass by (26), followed by 'Anarchy' on a white horse, 'like Death in the Apocalypse' rather than an individual agent (33). Shelley's use of 'anarch' and 'anarchy' is sarcastic. Milton used it of Chaos in *Paradise Lost* (II.988), but Shelley uses it of monarchs and monarchy, as if to say that any such rule is misrule. Besides that republican scorn Shelley adds the suggestion, consistent with the general strategy of the *Mask*, that monarchs only think they reign. Anarchy dresses himself up with crown and sceptre and leads 'the adoring multitude' in triumph (41). Lawyers and priests greet him in London and he is about to meet 'his pensioned Parliament' (85), when a 'maniac maid' named Hope, but looking like Despair, throws herself before the horses of Murder, Fraud, and Anarchy (86–101). It seems an act of suicide rather than, say, a petition for redress of grievances, and it foreshadows the willing expectation of death celebrated a little later. But, as Demogorgon told us, 'Hope creates / From its own wreck the thing it contemplates' (*PU* IV.573–4), and so an illuminated mist rises 'Like the vapour of a vale' (105) – a traditional symbol of prayer rising from the humble people – and turns into an armoured and winged Shape, with the morning star on his helmet. He must represent the collective hope of the people, or more precisely the recognition by the people that hope is something they share and therefore have the power to realize: 'Thoughts sprung' wherever the Shape steps (125). Anarchy drops dead off his horse and all his followers flee.

The ballad might have ended here, but Shelley decided to expand and specify just what the sacrificial act of the maiden means. So a song arises as if from the Earth, indignant over the blood of her children, addressed to the 'Men of England' and introduced with a stirring five-line stanza that also concludes it:

> Rise like Lions after slumber
> In unvanquishable number
> Shake your chains to Earth like dew
> Which in sleep had fallen on you –
> Ye are many – they are few.
>
> (151–5)

It reminds us in passing of Shelley's sleepy state before the news from Manchester woke him up, but it is less a projection of that arousal than the thesis implicit throughout *Prometheus Unbound* that the 'many' have only to awaken and the chains of tyranny will melt away. The 'few' have no intrinsic power. If the multitude adores them the anarchs will rule it; if not, they will evaporate like the dew, or like 'a dream's dim imagery' (212).

The first theme of the song is freedom, and indeed Freedom is addressed during a good deal of it. Under the rubric of Freedom Shelley includes Justice, Wisdom, Peace, Love, and well-being of every sort; they are all of a piece. The second theme tells Earth's plan for bringing it about. As *Laon and Cythna* and *Prometheus Unbound* were Shelley's restagings and rethinkings of the French Revolution, this poem is an ideal re-enactment of the Peterloo Massacre. 'Let a great Assembly be / Of the fearless and the free' (262–3) from everywhere in England, and as the workers at Manchester had hoped (the week before, in any case) to declare themselves an electoral body empowered to return delegates to a national assembly, let them 'Declare with measured words that ye / Are, as God has made ye, free' (297–8). Like the Manchester workers let them arm themselves only with the swords and shields of 'strong and simple words' (299) – like this poem, perhaps – and when the tyrants bring their artillery, their fixed bayonets, their horsemen's scimitars,

> Stand ye calm and resolute,
> Like a forest close and mute,
> With folded arms and looks which are
> Weapons of unvanquished war,
>
> . . .
>
> And if then the tyrants dare
> Let them ride among you there,
> Slash, and stab, and maim, and hew
> What they like, that let them do.
>
> With folded arms and steady eyes,
> And little fear, and less surprise
> ook upon them as they slay
> Till their rage has died away.
>
> (319–22, 340–47)

This is the crux. In Manchester the people fled in panic, but Shelley tries to imagine the effect on the soldiers and the English public if the people had simply stood there fearlessly and fallen willingly. As it happened, the popular revulsion helped galvanize the reform movement, but it was not to achieve even its partial success in 1832 without many further defeats. Shelley imagines the yeomanry and hussars returning in shame, pointed at by women and rejected by true warriors for whom killing unarmed civilians is contemptible, and then the rising of the whole Nation to shake off its chains.

Of Shelley's poems *The Mask of Anarchy* was second in popularity only to *Queen Mab* among the working classes in the 1840s and afterwards. The Chartist journals often quoted it, and it was often recited at public meetings. It may seem to be yet another instance of Shelley's incorrigible idealism that he could call on the workers to sacrifice their lives without resistance, but it did not seem naïve to the British workers themselves, whose long march to legal equality, the franchise, and a powerful Labour Party was accomplished with extraordinarily little violence. The Jacobin and Marxist-Leninist theorists of revolution have long criticized this sort of gradualism and patient self-sacrifice as defeatist or collaborationist or as a kind of pseudo-struggle unworthy of a militant proletariat, but the great revolutions on the Marxist-Leninist model have long looked like terrible mistakes, and statues of Lenin now lie in ruins like those of Ozymandias.

Shelley's vision did not seem naïve to a young Indian law student in London in 1888. Unable to eat most English food, he found the vegetarian movement and read its pamphlets, several of which quoted Shelley at length. The leaders of the vegetarians, whom he soon got to know, advocated a sweeping renovation of society by non-violent means. They loved Shelley; they were in touch with the Christian pacifist Tolstoy; they overlapped with the Fabian socialists, such as Shaw, who admired Shelley and went to meetings of the Shelley Society; they also overlapped with the Theosophists, who also took an interest in Shelley. Through all these circles the law student made his way. Years later, back in India, Mahatma Gandhi sometimes read *The Mask of Anarchy* aloud to his followers. If we are looking for a single source of Gandhi's notion of large-scale organized non-violent resistance, of *satyagraha*, we do not find it among the other works he loved – the Sermon on the Mount, the *Bhagavad Gita*, the essays of Tolstoy, Thoreau, Ruskin – but it is there, in full flower, in Shelley.

Epipsychidion

While living in Pisa in 1820, the Shelley household became acquainted with a remarkably beautiful and talented nineteen-year-old woman who was confined in a convent by her father, the governor of Pisa, while he negotiated for a suitable husband. Her name was Teresa Viviani, but Claire (who met her first), Mary, and Percy all referred to her as Emilia or Emily, perhaps in allusion to a heroine of Boccaccio's and Chaucer's in a similar situation. That situation appealed intensely to Shelley's long-standing mission to liberate young women from religious and familial tyranny, and he made a few indirect attempts to free this caged nightingale. There was little he could do, however, and within a few months a marriage was arranged. Shelley was ill during the time of his meetings and correspondence with Teresa and the feverish tone of his letters and the long letter-poem *Epipsychidion* may owe something to his illness, but he evidently fell in love with her and Teresa seems to have reciprocated in some way. The whole affair had a 'literary' quality to it (she also wrote poems of a traditional Petrarchan sort), as if it were a courtly love game or a sublimation of the feelings they shared of spiritual imprisonment. A fuss was made in her family over her intimacy with Shelley, and he worried about a possible fuss on Mary's part if she knew the extent of their communion, but it is unlikely that the two were ever alone together. Shelley's feelings for her, in any case, seem to have cooled even before her wedding day, for when he sent the poem to his publisher several months before it he wrote that 'it is a production of a portion of me already dead'. The 'Advertisement' published with it begins, 'The Writer of the following lines died at Florence'. Possibly the inevitability of her new confinement in an arranged marriage felt like the death of something inside him, but he was also thinking of his old theme, which we found in *Alastor*, of death as the gateway to reunion with ideal love.

Epipsychidion is in part a courtly love poem, not unlike the letters Teresa and Shelley exchanged, and it draws from the Dantean and Petrarchan tradition as well as the Song of Songs in the Old Testament. It is also in part 'an idealized history of my life and feelings', as he wrote a year later. It includes a famous passage that sums up his attitude towards legal monogamy, which some readers feel is out of place in a poem so deeply committed to one ideal love but which implicitly defends the poem as a whole against the charge of infidelity to Mary. And it ends with an escape on a boat to a paradisal island where the poet and Emily will consummate their love. Much of the poem has an epistolary and spur-of-the-moment air, as if the power and sincerity of Shelley's state of mind could only be poured out with unpremeditated art. He had recently been much impressed with an 'improviser' named Sgricci who could orally compose an entire five-act tragedy in verse, and it has been suggested that *Epipsychidion* is a kind of imitation of an improvisation, like Schubert's carefully composed impromptus. Certainly the apparent gush of feelings stands up less well to the kind of scrutiny that we can give to such earlier 'outpourings' as 'Mont Blanc' and 'Ode to the West Wind', yet as always Shelley's craftsmanship is on display.

The title is a Shelleyan Greek coinage, but its meaning is far from clear. The word *psychidion* is found in Greek, and it means 'little soul', the diminutive-*idion* suggesting endearment (like the '-ling' in 'darling'). In his brief essay 'On Love' Shelley wrote, 'We dimly see within our intellectual nature a miniature as it were of our entire self, yet deprived of all that we condemn or despise, the ideal prototype of every thing excellent or lovely that we are capable of conceiving as belonging to the nature of man.' 'Miniature self' would not be a bad translation of *psychidion*, and Emily certainly becomes an ideal prototype of love. When one adds the *epi-*, however, the meaning gets obscure. It cannot mean 'soul out of my soul', from line 238 of the poem, as some have argued, on the model of 'epicycle'. Nor can it mean 'About the little soul' or 'On the subject of the little soul', as most scholars now think, on the model of Latin *De Animula*, for *epi-* never means 'about' or 'concerning'. That may be what Shelley thought it meant, however, and it certainly suits the poem. It echoes the term *epithalamion* Greek for 'wedding song', and a wedding song is what it is, though the term means 'at the bedroom', not 'upon a wedding'. Though Shelley's title strictly means 'At (or near) the little soul', we might as well take it as the name of a Shelleyan genre, the 'soul song'.

The song is very self-conscious. It is framed within a preface and an envoy both addressed to 'My Song' or 'Weak verses', and the song proper refers to itself as 'These votive wreaths' (4) and 'This song ... thy rose' (9), 'this sad song' (35), and 'these flowers of thought' (384). That helps alert us to the artificiality of the tremendous surge of metaphors that sets the poem going. Emily is a captive bird, a Seraph of Heaven, and then

> Sweet Benediction in the eternal Curse!
> Veiled Glory of this lampless Universe!
> Thou Moon beyond the clouds! Thou living Form
> Among the Dead! Thou Star above the storm!
> Thou Wonder, and thou Beauty, and thou Terror!
> Thou Harmony of Nature's art!

and so on (25–30) in the exclamatory mode, followed a little later by another surge – she is a well, a star, a smile, a lute, a cradle, even a grave – in the interrogative mode (53–69). This breathless litany is so excessive that it defies criticism, as if to say that if we commented on its lack of coherence, control, and decorum we would only be confessing our deafness to the soul's music. I will none the less comment that each metaphor, no matter how original or well phrased, is diminished in the company of so many others, for if any one of them is adequate all the others are superfluous and if none of them is adequate the whole effort is futile. None of them is in fact adequate, of course, and the effort collapses: the poet seeks among the 'world of fancies' for 'one like thee' and finds only 'mine own infirmity' (70–71). Whatever she is, she so far exceeds his descriptive powers that she belongs to an absolutely transcendent, even ineffable, realm, as if she is the 'One' of Plotinus, about which nothing whatever may be said.

But this is a poem, and poems may not succumb to the ineffable or they cease to be poems. If we imagine for a moment that the poem itself is the speaker, then that threat of poetic annihilation may explain the opening of the next movement· 'She met me, Stranger, upon life's rough way, / And lured me towards sweet Death' (72–3). The poem picks itself up from the floor, however, and tries again for another round, calmer at first but growing frantic again –

> An image of some bright Eternity;
> A shadow of some golden dream; a Splendour
> Leaving the third sphere pilotless; a tender
> Reflection of the eternal Moon of Love . . .

– until it even calls her 'A Metaphor of Spring and Youth and Morning' when it has run out of metaphors (115–20), and collapses again: 'Ah, woe is me! / What have I dared?' (123 4). But the failures do not shake his fundamental article of faith, the truth that 'The spirit of the worm beneath the sod / In love and worship, blends itself with God' (128–9). The poet worm may fail to find words for the goddess Emilia, but its spirit somehow unites with hers.

The opening of the poem is somewhat obscure.

> Sweet Spirit! Sister of that orphan one,
> Whose empire is the name thou weepest on,
> In my heart's temple I suspend to thee
> These votive wreaths of withered memory.
>
> (1–4)

If 'that orphan one' refers to 'me', as seems likely (for he calls her sister again at 130, and wishes they had been twins of the same mother at 45), then it suggests the speaker is an outcast from his alienated home like the Poet of *Alastor*, and that his sole possession is his name. Emily weeps 'on' the name: that could be simply an archaic variant of 'weepest for' or 'weepest over', implying that she is weeping over losing him; the name, it has been suggested, is 'Percy', which sounds like the Italian for 'lost' (*persi*) in the plural. But there seems to be a glancing allusion to the balcony scene of *Romeo and Juliet*, where Romeo describes Juliet in the same extravagant terms Shelley finds for Emily (she is the sun, she is an angel, her eyes are stars) and Juliet laments on Romeo's name – his family name, not 'Romeo'. Emily, like Juliet, will be betrothed to another family by her father. The question of the name soon returns, though in equally obscure lines: 'Emily, / I love thee; though the world by no thin name / Will hide that love from its unvalued shame' (42–4). I am not sure what this means. The world, perhaps, will not allow him to give her his name, which would protect his love from great scandal ('unvalued' as 'beyond calculation'), or, what amounts to the same thing, the world will not legitimize the love by naming it 'lawful'. Since she is first named here, perhaps the name is 'Emily', a thin disguise for 'Teresa'; there had already been a fuss because he had not hidden his love under a plausible guise. In any case he goes on to wish 'that the name my heart lent to another / Could be a sister's bond for her and thee' (46–7): the name 'Shelley', now attached to Mary (but only 'lent', as if it might be returned to be lent to another), could become Emily's name, too, and she a second wife, the 'true' one if not the 'lawful' one (49).

To return to the opening: if the speaker imagines Emily as still weeping on his name, her memory of her loss still fresh, he implies that his own memory is 'withered'. The 'faded blossom' he offers her must be the faded love he felt but no longer feels, as if a part of him has died. They seem to be already banished from each other's company, for even though he addresses her throughout as if she can hear him and sends his verses to her in the envoy, he hangs his offering 'In my heart's temple', as if the poem is really only addressed to himself. And so, in a way, it is. But nothing seems faded or forgotten in what follows; it could hardly be more vivid or intense.

After a passage on the union of souls (130–46), Shelley then turns to the question of monogamy:

> I never was attached to that great sect,
> Whose doctrine is, that each one should select
> Out of the crowd a mistress or a friend,
> And all the rest, though fair and wise, commend
> To cold oblivion, though it is in the code
> Of modern morals, and the beaten road
> Which those poor slaves with weary footsteps tread,
> Who travel to their home among the dead
> By the broad highway of the world, and so
> With one chained friend, perhaps a jealous foe,
> The dreariest and the longest journey go.
>
> (149 59)

E.M. Forster found the title to *The Longest Journey* here; the passage had a beneficial impact on the long campaign to liberalize the British divorce laws. Its role in this poem may be less beneficial, though it is a relief from the desperate effort to address and define the goddess of love, and it serves as a transition to the autobiographical story of Shelley's love affairs. And of course it justifies the poet's wish (45–8) to have two sister-wives.

His first love affair is with 'a Being whom my spirit oft / Met on its visioned wanderings, far aloft, / In the clear golden prime of my youth's dawn' (190–92). Though described as female, she is not a real human being but a vision or dream revelation of the highest beauty: 'Her Spirit was the harmony of truth' (216). As if he had not yet learned his own lesson about selecting one mate out of a crowd, he is entirely drawn to his 'one desire' (219), but she disappears and leaves him desolate. She is not unlike the inconstant Intellectual Beauty except that her departure here seems final. During his despair a voice tells him 'The phantom is beside thee whom thou seekest' (233), and that sets him on a quest to 'find one form resembling hers, / In which she might have masked herself from me' (254–5). This is a variant of the *Alastor* quest, where the Poet sought the vision itself while neglecting the eligible maidens beside him. Here he will work his way through 'many mortal forms' until he encounters his original vision once again, and 'it was Emily' (344). His quest does not much resemble the upward progress of the soul that Plato and Plotinus enjoin us to undertake through mortal instances of love to the highest form of Love or Beauty; it is more a succession of failures ending in despair until Emily re-appears

Shelley had sufficient command of public decorum to see to it that the works he published, no matter how recondite, were in principle accessible to well-educated readers. Only a few passages, such as Ianthe's despair in *Queen Mab*, seem inadequately accounted for within the poem. The difficulties in the poems mainly arise from his having read everything, but everything he read was in the public domain and therefore fair game for allusions. Privileged inside information about Shelley's private life is seldom required as a key to interpretation. In the next passages of *Epipsychidion*, however, we seem to be left in the dark without that kind of information. (A similar case is the monologue of the maniac in *Julian and Maddalo*, which seems to refer to a terrible quarrel with Mary.) The passages raise interesting questions about literary method: is it fair to rely on information diligently exhumed by scholars to interpret a published poem? Can private meanings really be the object of allusions if no members of the contemporary public could possibly have recognized them? What does 'publishing' mean, and how is it different from, say, uttering something in everyday conversation or addressing a letter to a friend? How private was Shelley's private life anyway? When he writes an obviously confessional passage of a certain obscurity is he not inviting his readers to speculate and snoop around for pertinent gossip (even though he published the poem anonymously)? Must we rely on the notion of two audiences, a coterie and the general public, who understand two levels in the poem, an esoteric and an exoteric? Shelley wrote to his publisher, 'It is to be published simply for the esoteric few.' If so, where do we draw the lines between the two classes of reader?

It would take another book to discuss these issues properly. For now, I will only propose that it is worth trying to read the next passages of *Epipsychidion* both with and without the biographical allusions gathered by K.N. Cameron and others. Here are the probable allusions. 'One, whose voice was venomed melody' and whose 'touch was as electric poison' (256–9), may be a prostitute whom there is some reason to believe Shelley visited right after being sent down from Oxford. He became convinced he had caught a venereal disease and had never fully recovered; one of its symptoms, he thought, was his 'hair grown grey / O'er a young brow' (264–5). The One who 'was true—oh! why not true to me?' (271) might be Harriet Grove, whose loyalty to her family outweighed her affection for young Percy. Then

> One stood on my path who seemed
> As like the glorious shape which I had dreamed,
> As is the Moon, whose changes ever run
> Into themselves, to the eternal Sun;
> The cold chaste Moon . . .
>
> (277–81)

She must be Mary, who in her own letters called herself the moon; she and Percy seemed to have agreed that she is moonlike. She smiled on him and brought calm to his life, even laid him asleep (295), but he lay 'within a chaste cold bed' (299), sexually or at least spiritually unsatisfied. The astronomical scheme now holds for the next seventy-five lines or so: Shelley is the earth, 'This world of love, this *me*' (346), Mary the moon, and Emily the sun. Storms blotted the moon, and the 'Tempest' (312) seems to be another woman. 'She, / The Planet of that hour', is almost certainly Shelley's wife Harriet Westbrook, who 'was quenched' when she drowned herself (313); the Tempest might then be Harriet's older sister Eliza, whom Shelley blamed for their troubles. Storms, frost, and earthquake together might allude to the suicide of Fanny Godwin and the court's refusal to grant Shelley custody of his children by Harriet.

'At length, into the obscure Forest came / The Vision I had sought through grief and shame' (321–2), Emily, the Sun. She and Mary are now the 'Twin Spheres of light who rule this passive Earth' (345) and he asks them to continue to share their government in harmony with one another: 'Thou, not disdaining even a borrowed might', seemingly addressed to moon/Mary, shining with a borrowed light, and 'Thou, not eclipsing a remoter light' (362–3), probably addressed to sun/Emily. We hardly have a chance to doubt how long these joint regents might be expected to share power before another lady is invited home: 'Thou too, O Comet beautiful and fierce, / Who drew the heart of this frail Universe / Towards thine own . . . / Oh, float into our azure heaven again' where Sun and Moon will welcome her (368–79). That is certainly Claire, whose stormy relationship with Percy, Mary, and Byron seemed endless, and whose departure brought Mary, at least, some peace. (It is no wonder that Mary omitted to write a note to *Epipsychidion* alone among the major poems in her collected edition.)

Without the biographical references we must content ourselves with the detailed astronomical and meteorological vehicle for a rather vague tenor: something about Shelley's complex emotional experiences with women. Unsatisfying as that may feel, in the end it may be all we need to know in order to appreciate the main subject of the poem, which so far transcends all that sublunary turmoil that its details dwindle into insignificance.

The last movement of the poem is a dream-escape from the convent and a dream-marriage of two souls. 'The day is come, and thou wilt fly with me' (388). 'The hour is come: – the destined Star has risen / Which shall descend upon a vacant prison' (394–5). Love has the power to break our chains and burst our graves, and Shelley imagines the escape as a done thing. The remainder of the poem, almost two hundred lines, is one of the most beautifully sustained passages of love poetry ever written, and when one is caught up in it one entirely forgets that it is all hypothetical, all a wish. It touches our own wishes so deeply and gently (whether we are a man or a woman, I think), and it plays out our daydreams with such candour and control, that it seems to prove the premise of the poem: that a vision of love is inborn in us, and though storms may blot it out it will arise from a calm sea like Venus, 'Like echoes of an antenatal dream' (456). On a calm sea Shelley takes Emily in his boat to an Elysian isle, 'Beautiful as a wreck of Paradise' (423), where the Aegean kisses its sands and loving nightingales sing all day. There is perhaps a muted allusion to the ancient glory of Greece, now in a war with the Ottoman Turks for independence (which Shelley made the subject of his play *Hellas*). Sights, sounds, and odours are woven into perfect harmony, expressions of the island's buried soul. There is a dwelling built by an Ocean-King for 'his sister and his spouse' (492), with high towers and terraces overgrown with ivy and wild vine, where the poet and Emily will live a simple life with books and music and nature. They will wander in the meadows in the morning and retire to a cave at noon, where 'we will talk, until thought's melody / Become too sweet for utterance, and it die / In words, to live again in looks' (560–62) and then 'The fountains of our deepest life, shall be / Confused in passion's golden purity' (570–71) and they will blend into one. They will become 'one life, one death / One Heaven, one Hell, one immortality, / And one annihilation' (585–7).

With 'annihilation' the poem annihilates itself, as if thought's melody has become too sweet for utterance, but rather than leave us in an imagined consummation (like the end of Act III of *Prometheus Unbound*) it collapses abruptly and woefully. The poem itself seems aware of the fictiveness of its own subject, and like a dreamer who dreams he is dreaming it yanks itself awake.

> Woe is me!
> The winged words on which my soul would pierce
> Into the height of love's rare Universe,
> Are chains of lead around its flight of fire.
> I pant, I sink, I tremble, I expire!
>
> (586 91)

Shelley's fiction in his Advertisement is that the poet had expired after writing this, and so he had. He might have left us quietly in a calmly ecstatic state of mind before the 'Woe is me!' - he need not have feared that we would forget that this is only a fiction! – but then this putative poet would still be alive. Whether to square things with Mary or purge his passion for Teresa or enact dramatically the artificiality of this whole exercise in courtly love poetry, Shelley felt compelled to bring us back to earth with a jolt. An envoy, rather weak and anticlimactic, wraps things up. But however it dies, *Epipsychidion* has kept alive in its own little Elysium, after many passages of hopeless metaphor-launchings and embarrassing confessions, a serene but intense evocation of the human longing for a place of love and peace. That is flight of fire enough.

'To a Sky-Lark'

A few months before he met Teresa Viviani, Shelley wrote another outpouring on the subject of that great symbol of spontaneous musical outpourings, the skylark, and it has become one of his best-known poems: to many casual readers of poetry, Shelley has long been known above all as the ethereal lyricist of 'To a Sky-Lark'. In Livorno (Leghorn) in June of 1820, according to Mary, on a beautiful evening, she and Percy heard the carolling of a lark, and that inspired the poem which many readers have taken as a kind of instinctive warbling itself.

> Hail to thee, blithe Spirit!
> Bird thou never wert –
> That from Heaven, or near it,
> Pourest thy full heart
> In profuse strains of unpremeditated art.
>
> (1–5)

The fact that larks had been flying and singing through European poetry for centuries did not deter Shelley from writing another poem addressed to one of them. That Wordsworth had written a 'To a Sky-Lark' in 1807 ('Up with me! up with me into the clouds!') might even have been enough to inspire Shelley to try to surpass it, but the two poems are so different that it is unlikely we are meant to have Wordsworth's poem in mind. Closer in spirit is Wordsworth's 'To the Cuckoo' (also 1807), a few lines of which Shelley seems to echo: 'Even yet thou art to me / No Bird, but an invisible thing, / A voice, a mystery'. Also like Shelley's poem in many ways is Keats's 'Ode to a Nightingale', which had appeared in a journal in 1819, but it is not certain Shelley had seen it; when the volume containing it arrived in late 1820 he praised some of the poems but did not mention the odes. He might well have remembered, however, what Goethe's Faust tells his student: 'It is inborn in each of us / That our feelings thrust upward and forward, / While over us, lost in blue space, / The lark sings its thrilling song.'

Skylarks can sustain a loud, merry, musical song at great length while flying, and only while flying, and they sometimes fly so high that they can only be heard and not seen. These natural facts were enough to build the poem upon, and Shelley ignored the literary 'fact' that larks are morning birds, which Shakespeare relied upon for his famous debate between Romeo and Juliet over whether the bird they have just heard is the nightingale or the lark. Shelley heard the lark at evening, and so the time of the poem is that of 'the sunken Sun' (12), though 'the white dawn clear' (4) appears in a simile. However true to its occasion, the poem reads a little like a brilliant literary exercise, an exercise in sustaining, like the lark, 'profuse strains of unpremeditated art' (5) by means of similes and metaphors. And all those similes and metaphors, like those in 'Hymn to Intellectual Beauty' and 'Ode to the West Wind' before it and *Epipsychidion* after it, are meant to capture, or rather to fall short of capturing, the ineffable in words. If the first part of *Epipsychidion* is an attempt to convey the transcendence of visible beauty, 'To a Sky-Lark' is an attempt to convey the transcendence of audible beauty; if the one is an effort to name and define the goddess of love, the other is an effort to name and define the god of poetry. Beauty, Love, the creative and destructive wind, these are rather like muses of poetry; the bird is a poet himself.

Shelley may have meant the stanza form to seem unpremeditated as well as unprecedented. Its four short lines, rhyming *abab* (and with a tendency of the *a*-rhyme to be feminine or unstressed), are followed by a line twice as long, an alexandrine, that rhymes with the *b*-lines. The long line is often broken as if it were really two more short lines, but sometimes Shelley makes good use of its length, as in line five, just quoted, or 'Our sweetest songs are those that tell of saddest thought' (90); line 10 breaks in the middle, but only to link the two halves more effectively: 'And singing still dost soar, and soaring ever singest.' The short lines let Shelley get more rhymes in, that is, more 'music', while the long line lets him try for interesting rhythmical effects. I am not sure if the stanza is successful. If Shelley wanted to capture something of the sheer prolonged *sostenuto* of the lark then he ought not to have built the poem on short lines, for the single alexandrine is not enough to soar on. Something like Hopkins's wonderfully sustained syntax, in 'The Sea and the Skylark' (ignoring the outlandish diction for the moment) – 'I hear the lark ascend, / His rash-fresh re-winded new-skeinèd score / In crisps of curl off wild winch whirl, and pour / And pelt music, till none's to spill nor spend' – is very difficult to achieve if it has trimeter quatrains to straddle. Still, Shelley's poem has been dismissed so scornfully by influential critics as mere effusion that it is worth giving thought to its craftsmanship.

It is the string of similes, especially in the middle section where there are four successive stanzas beginning with 'Like', that has incurred the most scorn. What has a lark to do with a poet, a high-born maiden, a glow-worm, or a rose, and what besides their invisibility do they share? Their very invisibility, of course, is the point of the similes, and Shelley's task is somehow to express the invisible in things we can see. It is tempting to say in their defence that their very failure to do so only confirms the main point that the skylark's song surpasses all comparisons. As he did in the 'Hymn', in fact, Shelley resorts to a catch-all abstract category, 'All that ever was / Joyous, and clear and fresh, thy music doth surpass' (59–60). Yet he is usually quite resourceful in discovering equivalents to the feeling of not quite grasping the bird:

> Like a star of Heaven
>   In the broad day-light
> Thou art unseen, – but yet I hear thy shrill delight,
>
> Keen as are the arrows
>   Of that silver sphere,
> Whose intense lamp narrows
>   In the white dawn clear
> Until we hardly see – we feel that it is there.
>
> (18–25)

A morning star gleams ever more narrowly as its intense silver yields to clear white at dawn; at broad daylight it is invisible but we feel it is there; both birdsong and starlight, moreover, are like arrows, keen, shrill, and penetrating. Some of the other similes are just as well conceived individually, whatever their effect when strung together four or five in a row.

An early simile likens the bird to a Shelleyan poet:

> Like a Poet hidden
>   In the light of thought,
> Singing hymns unbidden,
>   Till the world is wrought
> To sympathy with hopes and fears it heeded not [.]
>
> (36–40)

It is interesting to see with what ease Shelley can deploy the two tradition-ally opposite birds to make the same point about poets, for in his *A Defence of Poetry* he writes, 'A Poet is a nightingale, who sits in darkness and sings to cheer its own solitude with sweet sounds; his auditors are as men entranced by the melody of an unseen musician, who feel that they are moved and softened, yet know not whence or why.' What the birds share, of course, is their invisibility, their reduction to pure bodiless voice. The lark, however, because of its notably high flight, lends itself better to Shelley's effort to convey by how much the transcendent perfection of the bird's song soars above human art. For having compared the bird explicitly to a poet, Shelley can begin the last section of the poem (61–105) by asking, as he might ask a human poet, 'What sweet thoughts are thine' (62) and what natural objects inspire it to sing (71–5). Human songs, whether 'Praise of love or wine' or 'Chorus Hymeneal / Or triumphal chaunt' (64–7), all classical forms that come closest to the unmixed happiness we hear in the lark, all have 'some hidden want' (70): a languor or annoyance, 'love's sad satiety' (80), false or shallow ideas about death (82–8), or 'Hate and pride and fear' (92). Even if we could overcome these things to which mortal flesh is heir, 'I know not how thy joy we ever should come near' (95).

We might note in passing an interesting contrast with Keats's response to the nightingale. Keats has been 'half in love with easeful Death,' as we have seen Shelley to be in several poems; Keats thinks it 'rich to die' at this exquisite moment of the bird's ecstatic singing. But he catches himself with the thought that, once dead, he would no longer hear the song that makes death desirable. He then claims that the nightingale is immortal: 'Thou wast not born for death, immortal Bird! / No hungry generations tread thee down'. Shelley will make a similar point in *Adonais* about ants and bees and swallows, the return of nature every spring and the seeming immortality of all natural creatures. In 'To a Sky-Lark', however, Shelley does not resort to the conceit that each individual member of an unchanging species is immortal. He makes the stranger claim, but a typically Shelleyan one, that if this bird is a poet it must understand what he, as a poet, has only glimpsed or speculated upon: 'Waking or asleep, / Thou of death must deem / Things more true and deep / Than we mortals dream' (81–4). Perhaps that truer and deeper understanding of death is what warrants the 'chrystal stream' of the lark's song (85).

Thomas Hardy, visiting Livorno in 1887, was moved to wonder where the dust of 'Shelley's Skylark', as he titled his poem, now lay. It seems as if he was replying to Keats as well as celebrating Shelley: 'The dust of the lark that Shelley heard, / And made immortal through times to be; – / Though it only lived like another bird, / And knew not its immortality'.

Shelley's poem expresses equally the joy of hearing the lark and the limits or failures of human effort to emulate it. If anything, I think, the balance tips towards joy and hope. There is certainly no collapse like that at the end of *Epipsychidion*, and the tone is more hopeful than that of the solemn final stanza of 'Hymn to Intellectual Beauty'. It is more in keeping with the ending of 'Ode to the West Wind', though less urgent and pleading, and with *Prometheus Unbound*, with which it was published in 1820.

> Teach me half the gladness
>   That thy brain must know,
> Such harmonious madness
>   From my lips would flow
> The world should listen then – as I am listening now.
>
> (101–5)

Shelley knows it is a futile wish, but its futility seems not to dampen his spirits much. It is as if the lark's song really has communicated its power to the mortal poem addressed to it, and as if the 'now' in which the poet is listening has lifted the poem out of the 'before and after' (86) of mortal time. Shelley may have felt that the decorum of a poem that ostensibly begins and ends during a lark's song requires that it sustain a lark-like theme and tone, even though the poem elaborates on the impossibility of achieving true larkhood. And Shelley may have felt buoyant rather than depressed that he had achieved what Hardy in his poem called 'Ecstatic heights in thought and rhyme' and what we might call a near miss at the impossible.

'Keats and Shelley' is still so common a phrase that many readers of poetry assume there was an intimacy, even collaboration, between them, as there was between Wordsworth and Coleridge. The pairing has official sanction in the Keats–Shelley Memorial Association in England and the Keats–Shelley Association of America. Both poets, it is widely known, were second-generation Romantics who died young about a year apart and were buried in the Protestant Cemetery in Rome (Shelley drowned with Keats's poems in his pocket), both wrote highly musical poems rich in imagery and metaphor, often in classical mythological settings, one is famous for an ode to a nightingale, the other for an ode to a skylark, and so on. But Shelley was no more than an acquaintance of Keats's (they had met at Leigh Hunt's) and had reservations about his poetry; Keats in turn had reservations about Shelley's; in fact they each advised the other to take a longer time and lavish more care on poetry, to 'load every rift of your subject with ore', as Keats said, quoting Spenser. Shelley seems genuinely to have thought Keats capable of great things, though he did not know all of the great things Keats had already written but not yet published. When he heard that Keats was ill with consumption, or tuberculosis of the lungs, Shelley wrote to him in July 1820 to invite him to stay with him at Pisa; Keats accepted, sailed for Naples, then went to Rome, and died there on February 23, 1821, without seeing Shelley. Shelley learned of his death in April, and almost immediately began an elegy called *Adonais*.

Shelley chose the ancient and highly conventional form of the pastoral elegy, two early versions of which, Bion's *Lament for Adonis* and Moschus' *Lament for Bion*, he had translated from the Greek. These in turn were inspired by the first Idyll of Theocritus (third century BC), who is credited with inventing pastoral or bucolic poetry (poetry about shepherds or cowherds), but they go back to ritual laments for the 'dying god', Adonis, traces of which we find as early as the songs of Sappho (sixth century) as well as Theocritus' Idyll 15. In naming the subject of his elegy Adonais, Shelley is evoking the origin of the genre, much as he tried to reconstruct and perfect the Prometheus myth. In the main version of the Adonis myth, the hero, a handsome young mortal, is beloved of Aphrodite, but he is gored by a boar while hunting and bleeds to death; from his blood springs a purple flower, the anemone. This is the version found in Ovid's *Metamorphoses* and Shakespeare's *Venus and Adonis*. In another ancient version, Persephone, Queen of the Underworld, also loves Adonis, and so a compromise is worked out between the goddesses whereby Persephone keeps him for one third of the year and Aphrodite for the rest. Both stories associate Adonis with the waning of life in the summer and its disappearance in winter. The festival of Adonis was celebrated in summer by women who cultivated little 'Adonis gardens' of pleasant herbs, made a lament before a statuette of Adonis, and then carried both the garden and the effigy to the sea.

The coined name 'Adonais', yet another odd Greek name to go with 'Alastor', 'Ozymandias', and 'Epipsychidion', may have recommended itself to Shelley because its metre, two trochaic feet, is a little easier to handle than that of 'Adonis'. Wasserman, however, has made the more interesting argument that 'Adonais' also evokes *Adonai*, the Hebrew word for 'Lord'. Adonis and *Adonai* have the same etymology, in fact, but the Hebrew echo suggests that Adonais will be more than a vegetation god who dies and is reborn. It was precisely such a god, under the name Tammuz, whose worship by women the Hebrew prophet Ezekiel denounced. Much of Shelley's poem is devoted to the question of whether Adonais is alive or dead and, if alive, in what manner.

In any case, Theocritus adapted the form of the lament to the death of anyone, or at least of any shepherd, while Moschus began the tradition of using the form to mourn the death of a fellow poet. In 1595 Spenser used it in *Astrophel: A Pastorall Elegie* on the death of Sidney, and in 1637 Milton used it in *Lycidas* on the death of King; to these precedents we may add Virgil's *Eclogues* and Pope's pastoral 'Winter' (1709). There was also a recent little tradition of laments for the 'boy-poet' Chatterton, who committed suicide at seventeen (1770). Coleridge wrote a 'Monody on the Death of Chatterton' (1790), Wordsworth mentions him with Burns in 'Resolution and Independence' (1802), and Keats himself wrote one of his first sonnets on Chatterton (1815); it has at least two images, the 'half-blown flower' and 'the stars / Of highest Heaven', that are found also in *Adonais*.

With all these intimidating precedents as inevitable comparisons, it is a wonder that Shelley managed to write anything at all. But readers today are more likely to be put off than impressed by the poem's artificiality or 'literariness'. Shelley himself called *Adonais* 'a highly wrought *piece of art*' and 'the least imperfect of my compositions', but one may ask, 'Is this any way to express one's grief?' and, 'Where is Keats in all this?' Well, Shelley may not have been stricken with grief by Keats's death, though he was certainly moved by it, but the first question raises a deeper one about the relationship of ritual to feeling. It is not beside the point to note that all societies have 'artificial' traditions of mourning that channel and contain the grief while at the same time drawing it out; there may be no 'natural' form of mourning at all. Shelley, too, understood from his study of the classics (though he sometimes seems to have forgotten) that emotion can be all the more moving for being expressed through strict and decorous forms. If we are less moved today, that probably reveals more about our own distance from the classical tradition than about Shelley's supposed insincerity. As for Keats, there are probable allusions to the time of year when he died, spring (in Italy) (136); to the way he died, a ruptured blood vessel in the lung, in the pierced breast of 152 and the five rhymings of 'death' with 'breath'; to a nightingale (145 and 372); to 'Dreams' as his flocks (73), his poems being even more dream-filled than Shelley's own; the change of scene to the cemetery in Rome; and the mention of Chatterton, to whom Keats not only wrote a sonnet but dedicated his longest poem, *Endymion*.

Keats is also present, however, in the form and style of the poem. Shelley had used Spenserian stanzas at great length in *Laon and Cythna*, but here, prompted perhaps by Keats's quotation from Spenser in the letter accepting his invitation, Shelley seems to salute Keats's use of them in *The Eve of St Agnes*, which was in the new volume of Keats's poems that Leigh Hunt sent to him in late 1820. (Spenser's own elegy on Sidney is not in Spenserians.) He also seems to have taken to heart Keats's advice to load every rift with ore. Shelley thought Keats had recently done the same thing in his *Hyperion*, his most Miltonic poem. To elevate Keats to a rank equal to Homer, Dante, and Milton, the three 'sons of light' (36), was a deliberate outrage in 1821, but it hardly seems outrageous today. Shelley's own poem helped place Keats among the stars. He could not bring him back to life, but he undid the damage to Keats's fame, as he saw it, by the harsh anonymous reviewer of *Endymion* in the *Quarterly Review*.

Aside from the Adonis myth, the murderous review is the major premise of the poem. Byron could not agree that Keats was killed by a bad review, and Shelley knew well enough the medical cause of Keats's decline and death, but there was indeed something callous and blind about the review and Shelley, smarting over similar reviews himself, wanted to strike a blow for a fellow outcast poet. The anonymous reviewer, the 'nameless worm' (319) and 'noteless blot on a remembered name' (327), Shelley was convinced, was his acquaintance the Poet Laureate, Robert Southey (it was not), but he prudently refrained from naming him. The decorum of the poem forbids it in any case, since neither Keats nor any living person is named, and the epigraph from Moschus in Greek ends with 'he escapes my song', as if to say he cannot be named in it. This critic corresponds to the boar in the original myth, a possibility Shelley must have relished, but to keep his anonymity before us Shelley makes him a stealthy archer who slays his quarry with 'the shaft which flies / In darkness' (11–12). That also lends point to his portrayal of Byron as an anything-but-anonymous counter-archer, indeed an Apollo with a 'golden bow' (249), who sent all the critics scurrying when he launched his devastating *English Bards and Scotch Reviewers*. It is a little disconcerting later when we are told 'Our Adonais has drunk poison' (316), but poison licenses the viper and worm imagery that Shelley must have found irresistible; it is also motivated by the *pharmakon* or poison twice named in the epigraph.

Instead of Aphrodite or Venus, who would not do as chief mourner of Keats, Shelley first tried 'Poesy' – we remember the cave of the witch Poesy in 'Mont Blanc' – and then decided on Urania, the highest of the nine Muses, patroness of astronomy (as befits the star imagery), and according to Plato the mother of heavenly as opposed to earthly love (*Symposium* 187d). She was also the Muse invoked by Milton at the opening of Book VII of *Paradise Lost*, so Shelley imagines her as Milton's widow, and as she could not 'defend / Her Son', the poet Orpheus, killed by Bacchantes (*PL* VII.32–9), Shelley asks 'Where wert thou mighty Mother, when he lay, / When thy Son lay, pierced by the shaft' (10–11); it follows that Adonais-Keats, 'The nursling of thy widowhood' (47), is the posthumous son of Milton. Urania has been sitting 'in her Paradise' (14), perhaps the kind of place Prometheus and Asia resort to after their reunion, where she has been listening to an Echo sing Adonais' songs. Urania is the first and 'most musical' (50) of mourners, but a long train of others join her: the Hour of Adonais' death, and other Hours; Dreams, one of whom speaks (84–7); a 'Splendour' (100), from Dante's *Paradiso*; Desires, Adorations, Persuasions, Destinies, and other spiritual or psychological states (109–16), summed up as 'All he had loved, and moulded into thought, / From shape, and hue, and odour, and sweet sound' (118–19); Morning; Echo; Spring, Ocean, and Winds; Phœbus and Narcissus; Albion (151), or England (a wishful thought); mountain shepherds; and 'one frail Form' (271). This long and heterogeneous list of allegorical personages tries the patience of some readers, but it is warranted by the tradition of pastoral elegy, which typically names a considerable roster of mourners, both to enhance the praise of the dead and to soften the grief of the living. This feature also suits, perhaps all too well, Shelley's distinctive tactic of piling on metaphors to embody a transcendent or ineffable subject, as we saw in *Epipsychidion*.

A frequent feature of the tradition is the participation of nature and natural creatures, both as mourners (here briefly as Morning, Spring, Ocean, and so on) and as a poignant contrast with mortality. For if we may console ourselves by conceiving that nature mourns our lost beloved, as if dying in sympathy with him, we cannot ignore the painful fact that nature also renews itself every spring no matter who has died. As Moschus states it,

> Ah, when the mallows perish in the orchard,
> or the green parsley, or the thickly blossoming dill,
> they grow again, and live another year;
> but we who are so great and strong, we men
> who are so wise, as soon as we are dead,
> at once we sleep, in a hole beneath the earth,
> a sleep so deep, so long, with no end,
> no reawakening. And so it is for you:
> in the earth you shall lie, shrouded in silence;
> whilst, if it pleases the Nymphs, a frog
> may sing forever.
>
> (trans, Anthony Holden)

Shelley's version of this theme begins what some critics take as the second movement of the poem (stanzas 18 through 38). The first movement implied that everything natural or spiritual is stricken with death, but now,

> Ah woe is me! Winter is come and gone,
> But grief returns with the revolving year;
> The airs and streams renew their joyous tone;
> The ants, the bees, the swallows reappear.
>
> (154–7)

All living things of nature come back, even lizards and snakes, and though we know that individual creatures do die, they seem to us unindividuated and immortal: it is the same frog croaking every spring. 'Nought we know, dies. Shall that alone which knows / Be as a sword consumed before the sheath / By sightless lightning?' (177–9). Why should the human mind or soul alone perish when everything that surrounds it like a scabbard lives on? (The 'sightless lightning' is the shaft of the invisible reviewer.) The returning life of spring succeeds only in touching the corpse for a moment and then leaving him 'in a most cold repose' (180).

Urania is finally roused to leave her 'secret Paradise' (208) and descend to the bier of Adonais, but all she can do is ask the futile question why and lament the ephemerality of godlike minds. Then the shepherds come (nearly the only strictly pastoral reference), all fellow poets: Byron first, then Thomas Moore, then 'one frail Form, / A phantom among men' (271–2) who is generally taken to be a self-portrait, and then Leigh Hunt. If the phantom is Shelley himself, however, we must wonder who the narrator is, who later speaks to 'my Heart' (469) and (probably) to himself as 'Fond wretch' (416). It may be better to take him as an Alastor-type, the outcast poet who mourns Adonais as the narrator of *Alastor* mourns him. Yet as the description continues –

> A pardlike Spirit beautiful and swift
> A Love in desolation masked; – a Power
> Girt round with weakness; . . .
>
> . . .
>
> His head was bound with pansies overblown,
> And faded violets, white, and pied, and blue;
> And a light spear topped with a cypress cone,
> Round whose rude shaft dark ivy tresses grew
> Yet dripping with the forest's noonday dew,
> Vibrated

(280–82, 289–94)

– he comes to resemble the god Dionysus (with his thyrsus), the god of tragedy and dithyrambic poetry, more than any individual poet. It is almost as if Poetry itself has come to mourn.

The third movement, if we can mark distinct movements, begins with a reversal, a clear assertion that Adonais is immortal after all: 'Peace, peace! he is not dead, he doth not sleep' (343). It is we who are dead in this realm we call life. If he seemed to be at one with Nature in their joint mortality, now 'He is made one with Nature' in immortality: 'there is heard / His voice in all her music, from the moan / Of thunder, to the song of night's sweet bird', the nightingale of which he so sweetly sang (370–72). This has a pantheistic ring, but then he seems to take part in 'the one Spirit' which governs Nature and makes it take on the forms of beauty (381), and that has a more neoplatonic sound. Since what is at stake here is Adonais' fame, his presence is both immanent and transcendent. He is still here among us, as we read his poetry and see the natural world through his eyes, yet he transcends us, not only in his rising fame (he is becoming a 'star') but in his godlike power of transforming our sight; he affects both what we know and that alone which knows.

As Adonais ascends to join the other immortal poets shining in the heavens, it is a little surprising that the speaker still feels disconsolate. No standpoint has satisfied him – not the universal grief of nature, not the resilience and forgetfulness of nature, not the forms of immortality Adonais achieves – for he is left alone in this life which is worse than death. ''Tis Adonais calls! oh, hasten thither, / No more let Life divide what Death can join together' (476–7). Earth and heaven are riven (491), and he is out at sea on his spirit's bark. The same image he used in praise of Wordsworth's former self, a star shining on a bark on a wintry sea, he invokes here to close the poem, but it does not sound hopeful or calm. Milton brings his pastoral elegy to a close with a twitch of his cloak and a shrug: 'Tomorrow to fresh Woods, and Pastures new.' Shelley, despite the movement of the argument through a complex development of ideas and imagery, seems to have gotten nowhere emotionally, and sets out not to new pastures, but on unknown seas, leading to death. The only way to be reconciled with death, it seems, is to join it. And so we are left as we are in *Alastor* with a deathward yearning, and it is only the existence of the poem itself, a highly polished work of thought and feeling, that offers us a counterweight to this despair.

Death triumphed over Shelley before he had finished his last work, *The Triumph of Life*. Its various manuscript fragments have been edited into a single narrative of about 550 lines, the general structure of which is fairly clear but many of the details of which remain mysterious. It breaks off, apparently at the opening of a new movement. How long it would have been, how it would have come to an end, how its many mysteries might have been clarified, we can only speculate. One speculation, however, we can rule out: that the poem was intended as a kind of farewell to life and poetry, as Shakespeare's *The Tempest* might have been. Though it seems to dwell on the meaninglessness of life and the relentlessness of death, and though Shelley had been fascinated with dying by drowning, the storm that capsized his boat was not conjured up out of his imagination. Two others drowned with him, and they were all on their way to meet Leigh Hunt and his family, who had come to Italy so Hunt could establish a new literary and political journal called the *Liberal* with Shelley and Byron. The despair that seems to dominate the poem, its apparent surrender of idealism or transcendental faith in favour of vivid but disconnected descriptions of the passing show, has attracted literary critics whose own despair is obvious. The famous deconstructionist Paul de Man concludes a long essay on the poem by stating its moral: '*The Triumph of Life* warns us that nothing, whether deed, word, thought, or text, ever happens in relation, positive or negative, to anything that precedes, follows, or exists elsewhere, but only as a random event whose power, like the power of death, is due to the randomness of its occurrence.' One wonders why anyone who believes such a thing would ever bother to write a poem, or even an essay about a poem. It seems unfair, in any case, that so many deconstructionists have triumphed over this poem, which was an incomplete set of fragments before they got to it. It is hard to resist the suspicion that they find Shelley's faith, hope, love, and revolutionary political commitments embarrassingly immature and threatening to their own comfortable nihilism, so that they congregate around *Alastor* and *The Triumph of Life* and other works where Shelley's own doubts or despair seemed for a time to overcome him.

T.S. Eliot, too, found 'greater wisdom' as well as 'better writing' in *The Triumph of Life* than in all of Shelley's earlier works, which were written by a confused adolescent. Besides the wisdom of despair, what seems to have attracted Eliot, the great admirer of Dante, is Shelley's Dantean mode and form, though presumably Eliot did not appreciate Shelley's use of the *Paradiso* in Act IV of *Prometheus Unbound*. Before Eliot himself Shelley was the greatest imitator of Dante in English. We saw how he used *terza rima* in a stanzaic form in his 'Ode to the West Wind', and how the example of Dante encouraged Shelley during his own Italian exile. *Epipsychidion* is filled with Dantean touches. In *The Triumph of Life* he returns not only to *terza rima* in its properly extended form but to something much like the setting and occasion of Dante's *Divine Comedy*. Indeed, much of the debate over the poem turns in part as to whether the main setting is a sort of hopeless hell or a kind of progressive purgatory.

In the Earthly Paradise at the top of the Mount of Purgatory Dante is privileged to observe an allegorical pageant or masque, indeed a triumph complete with a chariot drawn by a griffin, which embodies the texts and beliefs of Christianity and enacts the history of the church. At the end of it Beatrice commands Dante to tell what he has seen and heard 'to those / who live the life that is a race to death' (*Purgatorio* XXXIII.53–4). Shelley, who had already in *Prometheus Unbound* conveyed to mortals something like Dante's divine vision, may have been struck by Beatrice's phrase and decided to imagine what the earthly or perhaps infernal counterpart of the paradisal pageant might look like.

He sets his scene in a forty-line introduction that is more like a medieval dream-narrative than Dante's introductory canto in the *Inferno*, though it contains echoes of the latter. The first half of the introduction describes a natural setting as if it were a religious devotion. The sun rises suddenly and in splendour like a god, the 'smokeless altars of the mountain snows' (5) are set aflame, 'Ocean's orison' (7) rises (presumably the sound of his waves), the birds temper to it their 'matin lay' (8) or morning song, and the flowers swing their censers with incense that burns in the sunlight without being consumed, like the snow. Every mortal thing rises with the sun to begin the daily tasks he imposed on them long ago. To this universal praise and prayer, however, the narrator is alien: 'But I, whom thoughts which must remain untold / Had kept as wakeful as the stars' (21–2), now stretch out my limbs to sleep. He is the 'outcast man' of *Queen Mab* (III.199) who will not participate in the 'works of love and joy' that fill the universe. Indeed he literally turns his back on the rising god of nature and faces west over the sea towards the fleeing night. Dante also faces west as the sun rises, in the opening canto of the *Inferno*, and he too describes a mountain that catches the first rays of the sun. His attempt to climb the mountain, westward, is defeated by three wild beasts, whereupon he meets

Virgil, who will guide him the long way round, and down, to another mountain he will eventually climb. Shelley's narrator goes into 'a strange trance' (29) of *déjà vu* where all seems clear and glimmering with light and all seems a repetition of an earlier experience, perhaps a hint that he is repeating Dante's vision. Then begins his own 'Vision' (40), which occupies the rest of the poem as we have it.

The vision falls into two main sections: the narrator's account of the chariot pageant with the commentary on it by Rousseau (41–295) and Rousseau's account of his life and his own vision of the 'Shape' and chariot (296–543); a third section, introduced like the second with a question from the narrator, barely begins before the manuscript ends. The first thing the speaker sees is a vast stream of people, a multitude 'hurrying to and fro' (45) like gnats but borne relentlessly onward like leaves (two Dantean similes), much like the crowd that Dante sees in the vestibule of Hell where the cowardly and indecisive are punished: 'Behind that banner so long a file / of people – I should never have believed / that death could have unmade so many souls' (*Inferno* III.55–7). There is even less order than in Dante's multitude, as some seek what others flee and each interferes with another; they are all alike oblivious, however, to the fountains, forests, lawns, and flowers not far off the beaten track. Since it was these beautiful, natural things that the narrator also neglected, we have a hint here that the vision is meant to bring him back to them, just as Dante's vision puts him back on the path from which he strayed. But since we lack the conclusion, which might well have returned us to the initial setting, we cannot know if the vision will have a benign effect or if, like the vision sent to the Poet of *Alastor* for spurning the choicest gifts of human love, it will alienate the narrator further from the nature that rejoices all around him.

Neglect of nature, in any case, is not the main theme. He next sees a chariot shining with a glare intenser than the sun's but cold like the moon's, and bearing a 'Shape' with all the attributes of Death. Its chariot-eer has four faces like the four-fronted Janus, but blindfolded: it can see nothing in what has passed, what is passing (the two sideward faces), or what will pass (100–104). This charioteer resembles others in Shelley, such as 'The world's eyeless charioteer, / Destiny' in *Hellas* (711–12), but the chariot is very different from the ideal vehicle that carries Ianthe or Asia to the heights. This one is more like a juggernaut, which rolls over and crushes its dancing devotees; Shelley found a vivid account of a 'Jaga-Naut' in one of his favourite poems, Southey's *The Curse of Kehama*. But such a chariot invariably rolled in the actual triumphs of Imperial Rome – what we see is 'the just similitude / Of a triumphal pageant' (117–18) – as well as in the literary 'triumphs' that Shelley had been reading. The most important of these is Petrarch's *Trionfi*, a set of six allegorical triumphs (in *terza rima*) of Love over Man, Chastity over Love, Death over Chastity, Fame over Death, Time over Fame, and Eternity over Time. Petrarch fills the train of captives with famous mythological and historical characters, just as Dante peoples his three realms; one of them, in fact, is Dante, placed among the love-poets defeated by Love; another of Love's victims is Petrarch himself. The sequence of triumphs is progressive, building towards a heavenly consummation where Petrarch will be joined with his lost Laura. To the extent that Petrarch's work joins Dante's as a model, then, we have another suggestion that Shelley would have brought his own triumph to a hopeful conclusion.

The closest precedent in Shelley's own work is of course 'the triumph of Anarchy' in *The Mask of Anarchy* (57), also called a pageant (51), led by 'Anarchy, the Skeleton' (74) on horseback rather than in a chariot, but followed by 'the adoring multitude' (41) of deluded subjects. That whole masquerade is overthrown by the patient courage of the Men of England, and if the pageant in *The Triumph of Life* seems more intractable, more ingrained in the nature of things, that may be a delusion due to the incompleteness of the poem.

The chariot draws or drives everyone with it, 'till the last one' (133), rich or poor, powerful or weak, famous or infamous, with only two exceptions, those who 'as soon / As they had touched the world with living flame / Fled back like eagles to their native noon' (129–31), probably poets who died young, like Chatterton and Keats, and 'those who put aside the diadem / Of earthly thrones or gems', 'they of Athens and Jerusalem', Socrates and Jesus and presumably a few others, who spurned the temptations of this world (132–4). All the rest are caught up in a mad dance governed by sensual desires. The young ones dance in front, they drop, the chariot rolls over them, and not a trace of them is left behind; the old ones dance limpingly behind, they too drop, and disappear into the dust.

This 'sad pageantry' (as he mildly puts it) provokes the narrator to ask, half to himself, what it is, and whose 'shape' is in the chariot (176f.). A voice answers 'Life' and he turns to see 'what I thought was an old root which grew / To strange distortion out of the hill side / Was indeed one of that deluded crew' (182–4). This 'grim Feature' (190), a phrase Milton used for Death, has thin discoloured hair and holes that 'Were or had been eyes' (188) – he is apparently blind. He is, or once was, Jean-Jacques Rousseau, and he will serve as the guide to the pageant. Dante's guide was the poet Virgil, who was not only the paragon of philosophical reason but the greatest epic poet; he knew his way around hell because he had devoted the sixth book of the *Aeneid* to Hades. For Shelley to put

Rousseau in the same position, rather than a poet such as Lucretius or Milton, or a philosopher such as Bacon, is startling, and to make him one of the deluded crew, rather than a detached and superior observer like Dante's Virgil, is an interesting departure from Dante's model. The most unsettling aspect of Shelley's poem may indeed be the very absence of a trustworthy vantage point. When Rousseau tells his own story, acting the part less of a guide than one of Dante's sinners, we see very soon that he was just as baffled by his own life as the narrator is by the pageant.

Why Rousseau? As we trace it in his essays and letters, Shelley's estimation of Rousseau goes through changes, generally for the better, as he reads more of him, visits his memorial outside Geneva with Byron, and, perhaps, undergoes himself more of the passions and griefs that Rousseau recounts in his *Confessions*. That astounding autobiography shocked Shelley when he read it as a young man, and when he was nineteen he wrote in a pamphlet advocating an 'Association of Philanthropists' a dismissive couple of sentences: 'Rousseau gave licence by his writings, to passions that only incapacitate and contract the human heart: – so far hath he prepared the necks of his fellow-beings for that yoke of galling and dishonourable servitude, which at this moment [1812] it bears.' Napoleon, who is the first individual Rousseau will point out in the triumph (217–24), had turned revolutionary France into Imperial France, a copy of that Imperial Rome where 'Freedom left those who upon the free [of other nations] / Had bound a yoke which soon they stooped to bear' (115–16). The Rousseau of the poem takes no responsibility for Napoleon, but he admits that he ought to have forborne to 'join the dance' (189) and, while he claims that the divine spark that lit his spirit has lit in turn a thousand beacons (201–7), he also acknowledges that 'my words were seeds of misery' (280).

In his 'Essay on Christianity' (perhaps 1820), however, Shelley puts Rousseau on a loftier plane. After describing the origin of the inequality of mankind (in terms much like those of Rousseau's famous discourse on the subject) as a product of the excessive cultivation of physical wants, leading to a 'system of passions' by which fame, power, and gold are worshipped for their own sakes and the 'pageantry of empire' replaces the purpose empire might serve, he credits Jesus Christ with teaching the doctrines of equality, universal love, and simplicity and then adds: 'Rousseau has vindicated this opinion [the dogma of equality] with all the eloquence of sincere and earnest faith and is perhaps the philosopher among the moderns who in the structure of his feelings and understanding resembles most nearly the mysterious sage of Judaea.' *The Triumph of Life* distinguishes Christ (with Socrates) from nearly all others, but the Rousseauian dogma of equality may give us a standpoint from which to define what Rousseau the character calls 'Life': not life in a biological sense but life as led by nearly everyone under the system of passions that prevails in European societies, not life as subject to the inevitable corruption of the flesh but life as drawn into the unnecessary corruption of the soul. Multitudes may follow the chariot, but it is in the end by their own choice that they do so (Shelley is implicitly following Dante here, for whom sin must be freely chosen or it is not sin); a few do not. Though Rousseau himself did not escape the futile dance, he certainly implies that he might have, and there would seem to be little point in instructing the dreaming narrator if there is no escape for him either.

It is also interesting, finally, that in *A Defence of Poetry*, after praising Dante as the greatest poet of 'everlasting love', Shelley includes Rousseau among a list of poets – 'Ariosto, Tasso, Shakespeare, Spenser, Calderon, Rousseau, and the great writers of our own age' – who 'celebrated the dominion of love, planting as it were trophies in the human mind of that sublimest victory over sensuality and force', the triumph, in other words, of Love over Lust and the other deadly sins. The three times Shelley writes of Rousseau in his essays, we see, he thinks of him in the context of a triumph, though the virtue of the triumph reverses itself.

The narrator asks, 'And who are those chained to the car?' and receives a surprising answer: 'The Wise, / The great, the unforgotten' (208–9). They are there because they could not follow Socrates' command 'to know themselves' or, perhaps, Jesus' command to 'repress the mutiny within' (such as lusting in one's heart) (212–13). Rousseau then points out Napoleon, who sought to win the world and left it 'in its hope destroyed' (219); the sight of him fills the speaker with despair over 'why God made irreconcilable / Good and the means of good' (230–31). When the Furies showed Prometheus the terrible outcome of the hope-filled French Revolution he refused to despair, and Shelley in *The Mask of Anarchy* and many other places had already imagined precisely the means of good that would not defeat the good, so this feeling of despair, like those that overcome Dante several times in the *Inferno*, may be a sign that Shelley meant the speaker to be undergoing an education, a spiritual journey, like Dante's. Despair will yield to wisdom. There is little in the surviving text, admittedly, that indicates the way out of despair, but there is nothing in the text that precludes it either.

Despots appear next, and the philosophers who flattered them, all conquered by Life, while 'I was overcome,' Rousseau proudly adds, 'By my own heart alone' (240–41). We learn that Life conquered Plato's heart by love (in contrast to the conquering heart of Rousseau), Alexander conquered the world but darkened it as Napoleon would, his tutor Aristotle was 'throned in new thoughts of men' but is now supplanted by Bacon's spirit (science), which 'compelled' nature – one great figure after another Rousseau describes in the language of triumph and defeat (254–73). Even 'the great bards of old' are there, 'who inly quelled / The passions which they sung' (274–5). That triumph over themselves might seem to exempt them from the dance or race of Life, but their works were none the less infectious, like Rousseau's. Then a crowd of emperors, kings, and popes appears, whose only power was to destroy. Rousseau has made distinctions among the characters, but Shelley's allegory of the crowd and chariot is too general to allow him to make comparable distinctions in their conditions. In Dante's hell the nine circles with many subdivisions permit precise discrimination among sins and sinners – though of course all of them are in hell forever. (Only purgatory is a place of progress.) One can sense a struggle between the demands of the simple governing metaphor and the more subtle thinking of Rousseau the guide that might have brought Shelley to an intellectual halt. The key question becomes, 'What is Life?' and it is at just that point that the manuscript stops.

After the crowds of 'Anarchs' and popes, the speaker, 'sick of this perpetual flow / Of people', asks Rousseau where he came from, where he is going, and why (296–300). Nearly all the remainder of the poem is Rousseau's story, and its allegorical complexities are greater than any we have met so far. It begins in 'the April prime' (308), the beginning of the year, the season when Dante's poem begins and, perhaps, when this one does. 'I found myself asleep / Under a mountain' (311–12), much as Dante did – he had fallen asleep but then 'found myself' in a wood at the bottom of a hill. The mountain 'yawned into a cavern' (in an implicit pun on the cavern's 'mouth') out of which a gentle rivulet comes to water the grass and flowers, flowing with a sound that makes everyone forget all they knew 'before that hour of rest', especially the griefs they knew at the evening of another time (313–25). The rivulet is Lethe, the river of forgetfulness, which Dante places in the Earthly Paradise on the Mount of Purgatory (*Purgatorio* XXVIII.130 – Shelley translated the first third of that canto) and perhaps also at the exit from hell at the foot of the Mount (*Inferno* XXXIV.130). 'Whether my life had been before that sleep / The Heaven which I imagine, or a Hell / Like this harsh world in which I wake to weep, / I know not' (332–5).

There is no consensus over just what Rousseau is talking about here, and in much of what follows. The language is Neoplatonic and presupposes the doctrine of reincarnation. Shelley found no good evidence or arguments for belief in a pre-existent or future state, but he found it poetically irresistible, just as Wordsworth did in the 'Intimations' ode, where he wrote 'Our birth is but a sleep and a forgetting'. The cave would seem to be both tomb and womb, the place to which our souls go at death and from which they emerge at birth. Life is a sleep: our souls are encumbered with bodies, sensations, desires, distractions that obliterate pre-natal memory, and this oblivion is much like sleep. In the afterlife, before our soul's next incarnation, we are awake. But what is 'this harsh world in which I wake to weep'? Rousseau is literally dead in 1822, just as all the souls Dante meets are the souls of the dead, so the 'Hell' Rousseau now inhabits would seem to be the afterlife. But that runs counter to our usual sense of 'this . . . world'. The speaker cannot have gone back to the time of Rousseau's life, for Rousseau points out the recently deceased Napoleon (1821) among many others dead long before himself. Perhaps we 'wake to weep' midway in our life's journey, as Dante did, and as Rousseau seems to do later where the phrase is repeated (430). The ambiguities may be insurmountable as they stand, and there are so many of them that we doubt if Shelley could have resolved them all even if he had wished to. And he may not have wished to. The narrator himself, after all, falls into an ambiguous trance 'Which was not slumber' (30) at the time of awakening (4), though he has stayed 'wakeful' all night (22). If that ambiguity hints at later ones, the narrator's *déjà vu* also seems anticipatory, as if he has a premonition that *someone* will have already experienced what he is experiencing, or, even more uncannily, as if he senses that he is the reincarnation of Rousseau!

Yet it does not seem to be Shelley's purpose to tease us into metaphysical speculations about life and death and reincarnation so much as to chart the way 'Life' – this life as it is lived by most people in Europe today – lures and distracts us away from the ideals we held in youth. At 'broad day' in Rousseau's story, 'a gentle trace / Of light diviner than the common Sun' (337–8) remains for a while, like the 'clouds of glory' of Wordsworth's ode, which will 'fade into the light of common day' as we grow older. The sun's image burns golden on the waters of a well and shines green through the forest; on the floor of a fountain (seemingly from the well), amid the sun, appears

> A shape all light, which with one hand did fling
> Dew on the earth, as if she were the Dawn
> Whose invisible rain forever seemed to sing
>
> A silver music on the mossy lawn [.]

(352–5)

145

These beautiful lines, and many of those that follow, make the 'shape' seem benign. She glides along the river, like Dante's Matilda in *Purgatorio* XXVIII, and offers a glass of Nepenthe just as Matilda immerses Dante in the river Lethe in *Purgatorio* XXXI. (Nepenthe goes back to the *Odyssey*, where it is a benign drug that makes one forget one's griefs. Helen, a shape all light if there ever was one, offers it to Telemachus at IV.221.) Yet the forgetfulness she induces takes on a sinister tone: 'As if the gazer's mind was strewn beneath / Her feet like embers, and she, thought by thought, / Trampled its fires into the dust of death' (386–8). When Rousseau drinks the Nepenthe, or at least touches the cup with his lips, his mind becomes as sand on a shore, whose impressions are erased by wave after wave of the sea. Then the shape wanes and vanishes, though he continues to feel its 'obscure tenour' like a scent or soft tune or caress (412–33). Then 'a new Vision' (434) bursts on his brain in the aftermath of the Nepenthe: a chariot in a triumphal progress.

What does the 'shape all light' (352) stand for? Besides Matilda and Helen, she resembles Circe, another enchantress from the *Odyssey*, whose own potion turned men into beasts. (Circe is the daughter of the Sun, like the Shape.) She is much like the dream-maiden of *Alastor*, who also turns invisible but lingers over the death-drawn Poet. There seems to be good cause to allegorize her as Love, and perhaps instantiate her as Julie, the beloved of Rousseau's semi-autobiographical novel *Julie; ou, La Nouvelle Héloïse*, just as Dante's Beatrice is Love but also the real historical Beatrice. (Matilda is a kind of stand-in for Beatrice as Dante is preparing to meet her.) But Julie is a lower kind of love than Beatrice: it was sensual love that subdued Rousseau, according to this interpretation, and made him forget his higher calling. The Shape is then the earthly Venus, or Eros. But if that is true she is not so different from the shape in the chariot, Life, which blots her out just as she blots out the mind of Rousseau; since it is her Nepenthe, in fact, that raises the vision of the chariot, one might suspect they are in collusion. On the other hand, we might take her as the earthly love that leads us to a higher love, as Plato and Plotinus memorably argued (Shelley translated Plato's *Symposium*). That the Nepenthe leads to the grim vision may not be the fault of the Nepenthe or its owner, for the facts of life are what they are no matter what youthful ideals we imbibe. The chariot rolls on through the world, and we are compelled to deal with it one way or the other.

Some critics have taken the Shape as the Muse, or as imagination, or even, most abstractly, as 'the figure of all figuration', all of which shifts the weight of the poem from a study of life in all its ramifications (including religion and politics) to a self-conscious meditation on the condition of poetry itself, or of figurative language. Whatever insights this thesis may yield, in my view, it blots out the life of the poem to take its *subject* as the difficulty of writing about life. Shelley was a self-conscious poet, no doubt (so was Dante), but he did not anticipate certain contemporary critics' obsession with the impossibility of saying anything unambiguous. It is simpler, in any case, to leave the Shape somewhat ambiguous than to 'resolve' it into a theory about ambiguity itself.

The new chariot is more or less a reprise of the old one, except that in Rousseau's time the chariot comes with 'savage music, stunning music' (435), which may or may not be a significant difference. It is the same multitude swirling around it, the same futility and anarchy. Rousseau says that he was not delayed long by flowers or by 'the phantom of that early form', the Shape (464), from plunging, in a gesture that seems both heroic and desperate, into 'The thickest billows of the living storm' (466). Before the chariot approaches the 'opposing steep' of the valley – as if nearing the end of Rousseau's life – a new vision or 'wonder' appears (470–71). If I seem to have discussed Dante too often in this chapter, my defence is Rousseau's next lines, where he himself invokes the poet whom 'Love led serene' through Hell, Purgatory, and Heaven, and who returned to tell 'How all things are transfigured, except Love' (471–6). If the world of Shelley's poem seems bleak and hopeless, if even the figure of love seems only to betray us to life rather than to draw us above it, the example of Dante reminds us that this is not the whole story, not the whole of life or love. 'The world can hear not the sweet notes that move / The sphere whose light is melody to lovers' (478–9): the music of the sphere transcends the hearing of the wrathful 'world' but lovers can see its light as if it were the music.

The new wonder is a great flock of phantoms, gathered like vampire bats, that darken the earth. These seem to represent the ideas or ideologies that prevail over the world, especially in these dark times, and they are recognizably the ones Shelley has been denouncing consistently since before *Queen Mab*: the ideas play with kingly and papal gewgaws, such as 'the crown which girt with empire / A baby's or an idiot's brow' (498–9), a clear enough allusion to the infant son of Napoleon, who was made King of Rome in 1811, and the late King George III of England, who reigned in his dotage. Another passage may refer to the restored Bourbons and the other ancient houses of Europe. Other phantoms, less specific, 'like discoloured flakes of snow / On fairest bosoms and the sunniest hair / Fell, and were melted by the youthful glow / Which they extinguished' (511–14), freezing the hopes of ardent idealists like the young Rousseau and – if the pessimistic critics are right – the young Shelley: 'and in the eyes where once hope shone / Desire like a lioness bereft / Of its last cub, glared ere it died' (524–6).

It is premature, however, and will remain forever premature, to conclude that Shelley's poem is the last glare of his dying hope, for a new movement is launched at the end of the manuscript which would seem, on formal grounds alone, unlikely simply to repeat the lessons of the first two versions of the chariot and its triumph. Since the poem makes use only of the first of Petrarch's *Trionfi* it is reasonable to guess that Shelley envisaged a much longer poem. Among his papers no outline or statement of his intentions has been found, and Mary Shelley wrote no note for it, so speculation has few solid barriers to check its career. I think the evidence is against the nihilistic readings of the present age, which would turn the poem into an example of a scepticism far beyond anything Shelley had advocated, and against self-referential readings, which would turn this poem as it turns all poems into a parable about itself. Both these interpretations, which reinforce each other, wrench the poem from the historical setting made manifest in its many allusions to recent events and current evils.

The Romantic movement elevated the fragment to great prestige. Some poems, such as Coleridge's 'Kubla Khan' and *Christabel*, were published unfinished by their authors, who thereby gave them a somewhat different status from fragments dug out of the papers of a poet who died before he had abandoned them. Shelley never sent anything unfinished to the press. Indeed he was renowned for the care he lavished on the details of his works, as even several of his political enemies acknowledged. Like the ancient and medieval ruins that Shelley and the other Romantics loved to haunt, the ruin of *The Triumph of Life* gives a kind of melancholy meditative pleasure. As long as we remember that it *is* incomplete, by a poet not yet thirty, and it is not a definitive final statement by an old man looking back on his career, Shelley would not begrudge us the endless speculation it affords on the meaning of life, and of death.

Appendix of Quotations

To Percy Shelley
On the Degrading Notions of Deity

What wonder, Percy, that with jealous rage
  Men should defame the kindly and the wise,
  When in the midst of the all-beauteous skies,
And all this lovely world, that should engage
Their mutual search for the old golden age,
  They seat a phantom, swelled into grim size
  Out of their own passions and bigotries,
And then, for fear, proclaim it meek and sage!

And this they call a light and a revealing!
  Wise as the clown, who plodding home at night
  In autumn, turns at call of fancied elf,
And sees upon the fog, with ghastly feeling,
  A giant shadow in its imminent might,
  Which his own lanthorn throws up from himself.

Leigh Hunt (1818)

He [Scythrop] now became troubled with the *passion for reforming the world*. He built many castles in the air, and peopled them with secret tribunals, and bands of illuminati, who were always the imaginary instruments of his projected regeneration of the human species. As he intended to institute a perfect republic, he invested himself with absolute sovereignty over these mystical dispensers of liberty. He slept with Horrid Mysteries under his pillow, and dreamed of venerable eleutherarchs and ghastly confederates holding midnight conventions in subterranean caves. He passed whole mornings in his study, immersed in gloomy reverie, stalking about the room in his nightcap, which he pulled over his eyes like a cowl, and folding his striped calico dressing-gown about him like the mantle of a conspirator.

'Action,' thus he soliloquized, 'is the result of opinion, and to new-model opinion would be to new-model society. Knowledge is power; it is in the hands of a few, who employ it to mislead the many, for their own selfish purposes of aggrandizement and appropriation. What if it were in the hands of a few who should employ it to lead the many? What if it were universal, and the multitude were enlightened? No. The many must always be in leading-strings; but let them have wise and honest conductors. A few to think, and many to act; that is the only basis of perfect society. So thought the ancient philosophers: they had their esoterical and exoterical

149

doctrines. So thinks the sublime Kant, who delivers his oracles in language which none but the initiated can comprehend. Such were the views of those secret associations of illuminati, which were the terror of superstition and tyranny, and which, carefully selecting wisdom and genius from the great wilderness of society, as the bee selects honey from the flowers of the thorn and the nettle, bound all human excellence in a chain, which, if it had not been prematurely broken, would have commanded opinion, and regenerated the world.'

Scythrop proceeded to meditate on the practicability of reviving a confederation of regenerators. To get a clear view of his own ideas, and to feel the pulse of the wisdom and genius of the age, he wrote and published a treatise, in which his meanings were carefully wrapped up in the monk's hood of transcendental technology, but filled with hints of matter deep and dangerous, which he thought would set the whole nation in a ferment; and he awaited the result in awful expectation, as a miner who has fired a train awaits the explosion of a rock. However, he listened and heard nothing; for the explosion, if any ensued, was not sufficiently loud to shake a single leaf of the ivy on the towers of Nightmare Abbey; and some months afterwards he received a letter from his bookseller, informing him that only seven copies had been sold, and concluding with a polite request for the balance.

Thomas Love Peacock, *Nightmare Abbey* (1818)

You will have heard by this time that Shelley and another gentleman (Captain Williams) were drowned about a month ago (a *month* yesterday), in a squall off the Gulf of Spezia. There is thus another man gone, about whom the world was ill-naturedly, and ignorantly, and brutally mistaken. It will, perhaps, do him justice *now*, when he can be no better for it . . .

We have been burning the bodies of Shelley and Williams on the sea-shore, to render them fit for removal and regular interment. You can have no idea what an extraordinary effect such a funeral pile has, on a desolate shore, with mountains in the back-ground and the sea before, and the singular appearance the salt and frankincense gave to the flame. All of Shelley was consumed, except his *heart*, which would not take the flame, and is now preserved in spirits of wine.

Lord Byron, two letters to Thomas Moore, 8 and 27 August, 1822

Shelley, the writer of some infidel poetry, has been drowned; *now* he knows whether there is a God or no.

Notice in the *Courier* (1822)

[Shelley] is one of the best *artists* of us all: I mean in workmanship of style.

William Wordsworth (1827?), from Christopher Wordsworth, *Memoirs*, II, p. 474

Shelley was a man of great power as a poet, and could he only have had some notion of order, could you only have given him some plane whereon to stand, and look down upon his own mind, he would have succeeded. There are flashes of the true spirit to be met with in his works. Poor Shelley, it is a pity I often think that I never met with him. I could have done him good. He went to Keswick on purpose to see me and unfortunately fell in with Southey instead. There could have been nothing so unfortunate. Southey had no understanding for a toleration of such principles as Shelley's.

I should have laughed at his Atheism. I could have sympathized with him and shown him that I did so, and he would have felt that I did so. I could have shown him that I had once been in the same state myself, and I could have guided him through it. I have often bitterly regretted in my heart of hearts that I did never meet with Shelley.

Samuel Taylor Coleridge (1830), in conversation

Shelley, though a poetic mind, is never a poet. His muse is uniformly imitative; all his poems composite. A good English scholar he is, with ear, taste, and memory, much more, he is a character full of noble and prophetic traits; but imagination, the original, authentic fire of the bard, he has not. He is clearly modern, and shares with Richter, Chateaubriand, Manzoni, and Wordsworth, the feeling of the infinite, which so labors for expression in their different genius. But all his lines are arbitrary, not necessary.

Ralph Waldo Emerson, 'Thoughts on Modern Literature' (1840)

I would take Shelley, and take him, not in his more matured state, but in his poetic boyhood, when he was inditing the fierce and ponderous commentaries of *Queen Mab*; take him in his hostility to our received forms of faith and received authorities; take him when in the first fervour of youth, he was throwing down the gauntlet to every species of superstition, and waging against theology an interminable warfare; and I say, that even at that moment, Shelley was a religious poet. Whatever is just, true, and beautiful in human feelings, as it flows out toward the vast universe of which we are a portion – whatever is most ennobling and divine in the principle of love toward all beings – whatever tends to show the advance in human nature, and even in unconscious being – we have in that persecuted and condemned 'Queen Mab' a demonstration that if Shelley were an atheist, he was an atheist whom a God might love, and in whom we may perceive a brother, who, by the fraternal affection that binds the race together, would point the aspirations of that race upwards, toward whatever is most true, beautiful, sublime, and enduring; and if that be not religion, there is no religion on the face of the earth.

W.J. Fox, in the *People's Journal* (7 March 1846)

Memorabilia

Ah, did you once see Shelley plain,
    And did he stop and speak to you
And did you speak to him again?
    How strange it seems and new!

151

But you were living before that,
    And also you are living after;
And the memory I started at –
    My starting moves your laughter.

I crossed a moor, with a name of its own
    And a certain use in the world no doubt,
Yet a hand's-breadth of it shines alone
    'Mid the blank miles round about:

For there I picked up on the heather
    And there I put inside my breast
A moulted feather, an eagle-feather!
    Well, I forget the rest.

Robert Browning (c. 1851)

Percy Bysshe Shelley
(Inscription for the couch, still preserved,
on which he passed the last night of his life.)

'Twixt those twin worlds – the world of Sleep, which gave
No dream to warm, the tidal world of Death,
Which the earth's sea, as the earth, replenisheth –
Shelley, Song's orient sun, to breast the wave,
Rose from his couch that morn. Ah! did he brave
Only the sea? – or did man's deed of hell
Engulf his bark 'mid mists impenetrable? . . .
No eye discerned, nor any power might save.
When that mist cleared, O Shelley! what dread veil
Was rent for thee, to whom far-darkling Truth
Reigned sovereign guide through thy brief ageless youth?
Was the Truth *thy* Truth, Shelley? – Hush! All-Hail,
Past doubt, thou gav'st it; and in Truth's bright sphere
Art first of praisers, being most praised here.

Dante Gabriel Rossetti (1870)

Poor Shelley always was, and is, a kind of ghastly object; colourless, pallid, tuneless, without health or warmth or vigour; the sound of him shrieky, frosty, as if a *ghost* were trying to 'sing' to us; the temperament of him, spasmodic, hysterical, instead of strong or robust; with fine affectations and aspirations, gone all such a road – a man infinitely too *weak* for the solitary scaling of the Alps which he undertook in spite of all the world.

Thomas Carlyle, *Reminiscences* (published 1881)

The man Shelley, in very truth, is not entirely sane, and Shelley's poetry is not entirely sane either. The Shelley of actual life is a vision of beauty and radiance, indeed, but availing nothing, effecting nothing. And in poetry, no less than in life, he is 'a beautiful and *ineffectual* angel, beating in the void his luminous wings in vain.'

Matthew Arnold, 'Shelley' (1888)

I have heard my father [Karl Marx] and Engels again and again speak of this [Shelley's influence on the Chartist Movement]; and I have heard the same from the many Chartists it has been my good fortune to know as a child and young girl – Ernest Jones, Richard Moore, the Watsons, George Julian Harney, and others. Only a very few months ago, I heard Harney and Engels talking of the Chartist times, and of the Byron- and especially Shelley-worship of the Chartists; and on Sunday last Engels said: 'Oh, we all knew Shelley by heart then.' Surely to have been one of the inspirers of such a movement isn't bad for an 'ineffectual angel' and 'Dreamer'.

Eleanor Marx (1892)

So if we outline our relationship to Shelley from the vantage ground of 1927 we shall find that his England is a barbarous place where they imprison journalists for being disrespectful to the Prince Regent, stand men in stocks for publishing attacks upon the Scriptures, execute weavers upon the suspicion of treason, and, without giving proof of strict religious belief themselves, expel a boy from Oxford for avowing his atheism. Politically, then, Shelley's England has already receded, and his fight, valiant though it is, seems to be with monsters who are a little out of date, and therefore slightly ridiculous. But privately he is much closer to us. For alongside the public battle wages, from generation to generation, another fight which is as important as the other, though much less is said about it. Husband fights with wife and son with father. The poor fight the rich and the employer fights the employed. There is a perpetual effort on the one hand to make all these relationships more reasonable, less painful and less servile; on the other, to keep them as they are. Shelley, both as son and as husband, fought for reason and freedom in private life, and his experiments, disastrous as they were in many ways, have helped us to greater sincerity and happiness in our own conflicts. The Sir Timothys of Sussex are no longer so prompt to cut their sons off with a shilling; the Booths and the Baxters are no longer quite so sure that an unmarried wife is an unmitigated demon. The grasp of convention upon private life is no longer quite so coarse or quite so callous because of Shelley's successes and failures.

Virginia Woolf, 'Not One of Us' (1927)

153

Critical Studies: The Poetry of Shelley

The ideas of Shelley seem to me always to be ideas of adolescence   as there is every reason why they should be. And an enthusiasm for Shelley seems to me also to be an affair of adolescence: for most of us, Shelley has marked an intense period before maturity, but for how many does Shelley remain the companion of age? I confess that I never open the volume of his poems simply because I want to read poetry, but only with some special reason for reference. I find his ideas repellent; and the difficulty of separating Shelley from his ideas and beliefs is still greater than with Wordsworth.

T.S. Eliot, from *The Use of Poetry and the Use of Criticism* (1933)

There are senile and vulgar illusions no less than illusions adolescent and heroical; and of the two, I see no reason for preferring the former.

C.S. Lewis, from 'Shelley, Dryden, and Mr. Eliot', in *Selected Literary Essays* (1939)

No stupider judgement was ever passed upon Shelley than by Arnold who called him an 'ineffectual angel'. There spoke the school-inspector who believes that 'good' is something done by busy people. Giving men material goods and material aid can not make them better, only better off; the effect of poetry is to change us permanently in our nature; a transmutation by no means ineffectual. It would be hard to name a poet whose political and social propaganda – to put it at its lowest has more effectively changed public opinion and altered the course of history. More far-reaching is the transforming power of poetry itself. Only those lacking in all sensibility to a poetry which speaks to the soul in its own language and of its native place and state can read Shelley unchanged.

Kathleen Raine, from *Defending Ancient Springs* (1967)

Further Reading

Editions

Two hundred years after Shelley's birth there is still no adequate complete edition of his poetry, prose, or letters. Both for students reading Shelley the first time and for scholars needing an accurate edition, the best book to own is Donald H. Reiman and Sharon B. Powers, eds, *Shelley's Poetry and Prose* (New York and London: Norton, 1977). It contains all of the poems discussed in this book and many more; they are carefully edited from the manuscripts and first editions and well annotated. *A Defence of Poetry* is included complete, along with two shorter essays. Though this is a paperback 'student' edition it is the standard for scholars as well. A second book worth owning is Thomas Hutchinson, ed., *The Complete Poetical Works of Percy Bysshe Shelley* in the Oxford Standard Authors series, first published in 1905 and lightly revised in 1970 by G.M. Matthews. It contains all the poetry known by 1905, including *The Revolt of Islam* [*Laon and Cythna*] complete, which Reiman and Powers omit. It is available in paperback in Britain but not, as of 1992, in the United States.

Scholars often cite the ten-volume 'Julian Edition' of the *Complete Works of Percy Bysshe Shelley*, edited by Roger Ingpen and Walter E. Peck (1926–30), because it included all the known poetry, prose, and letters, but it is not properly edited. Two volumes of a planned four of the Oxford English Texts edition, edited by Neville Rogers, have appeared (1972, 1975), but they were greeted with so much criticism by other scholars that Oxford has withdrawn them. The edition we have been waiting for seems to be arriving at last: *The Poems of Shelley* in the Longmans Annotated English Poets series, edited by Geoffrey Matthews and Kelvin Everest; the first volume, which goes a little beyond 'Mont Blanc', appeared in 1989. It is very scrupulously edited, with thorough annotations and variants. Two more volumes are projected, but it may take more than two. It is to be hoped that it will be made available in paperback, volume by volume, for the hardcover version is very expensive.

There are a number of inexpensive selected editions of Shelley's verse, but most of them include only parts of *Prometheus Unbound*, his most important long work, and some of them are based on older inadequately edited collected editions. The best of these is Timothy Webb, ed., *Shelley: Selected Poems* for the Everyman series (1977).

David Lee Clark's one-volume edition of *Shelley's Prose* (Albuquerque: University of New Mexico, 1954) is virtually complete but quirkily annotated. A scholarly edition, edited by E.B. Murray and Timothy Webb, is under way for Oxford. The letters are available in Frederick L. Jones's edition (1964), but these too need re-editing.

Biographies

The standard scholarly biography for twenty-five years was Newman Ivey White, *Shelley* (1940, revised 1947). It was partly superseded by Richard Holmes, *Shelley: The Pursuit* (1974), which has new material and interesting interpretations of some episodes of Shelley's life but emphasizes its weird and crotchety side. White's full and judicious if less exciting version remains important. Also very good is Part One of Kenneth Neill Cameron, *Shelley: The Golden Years* (1974), which summarizes his life from 1814 to his death. William St Clair, *The Godwins and the Shelleys: The Biography of a Family* (1989), is a fascinating and deeply researched study, and delightfully written, but somewhat mistitled: it is really a biography of Shelley's father-in-law William Godwin with a good deal about the Shelleys and Mary Wollstonecraft.

Criticism

The most profound and systematic interpretation of Shelley is Earl R. Wasserman, *Shelley: A Critical Reading* (1971), which incorporates chapters from *The Subtler Language* (1959) and his book *Shelley's 'Prometheus Unbound'* (1965). It is a demanding book, but lucid and jargon-free throughout. Most criticism since Wasserman has been, as it must be, in dialogue with him.

A good introduction to Shelley is Timothy Webb, *Shelley: A Voice Not Understood* (1977). Also useful to new readers is David B. Pirie, *Shelley*, for the Open University Press (1988). The best recent discussion of his distinctive poetic means is William Keach, *Shelley's Style* (1984). There are several good studies of the social and political dimension of his work: Kenneth Neill Cameron, *The Young Shelley: Genesis of a Radical* (1950) and *Shelley: The Golden Years* (1974); P.M.S. Dawson, *The Unacknowledged Legislator: Shelley and Politics* (1980); and Michael Scrivener, *Radical Shelley: The Philosophical Anarchism and Utopian Thought of Percy Bysshe Shelley* (1982). There are so many other books and articles worth reading that I will not try to list them here. For an assessment of them up to 1984 see the section on Shelley by Stuart Curran in *The English*

Further Reading

Romantic Poets: A Review of Research and Criticism, Fourth Edition, edited by Frank Jordan, published by the Modern Language Association of America (1985).

Discover more about our forthcoming books through Penguin's FREE newspaper...

Penguin

Quarterly

It's packed with:

- exciting features
- author interviews
- previews & reviews
- books from your favourite films & TV series
- exclusive competitions & much, much more...

Write off for your free copy today to:
Dept JC
Penguin Books Ltd
FREEPOST
West Drayton
Middlesex
UB7 0BR
NO STAMP REQUIRED

READ MORE IN PENGUIN

In every corner of the world, on every subject under the sun, Penguin represents quality and variety – the very best in publishing today.

For complete information about books available from Penguin – including Puffins, Penguin Classics and Arkana – and how to order them, write to us at the appropriate address below. Please note that for copyright reasons the selection of books varies from country to country.

In the United Kingdom: Please write to *Dept. JC, Penguin Books Ltd, FREEPOST, West Drayton, Middlesex UB7 OBR*

If you have any difficulty in obtaining a title, please send your order with the correct money, plus ten per cent for postage and packaging, to *PO Box No. 11, West Drayton, Middlesex UB7 OBR*

In the United States: Please write to *Penguin USA Inc., 375 Hudson Street, New York, NY 10014*

In Canada: Please write to *Penguin Books Canada Ltd, 10 Alcorn Avenue, Suite 300, Toronto, Ontario M4V 3B2*

In Australia: Please write to *Penguin Books Australia Ltd, 487 Maroondah Highway, Ringwood, Victoria 3134*

In New Zealand: Please write to *Penguin Books (NZ) Ltd, 182–190 Wairau Road, Private Bag, Takapuna, Auckland 9*

In India: Please write to *Penguin Books India Pvt Ltd, 706 Eros Apartments, 56 Nehru Place, New Delhi 110 019*

In the Netherlands: Please write to *Penguin Books Netherlands B.V., Keizersgracht 231 NL–1016 DV Amsterdam*

In Germany: Please write to *Penguin Books Deutschland GmbH, Friedrichstrasse 10–12, W–6000 Frankfurt/Main 1*

In Spain: Please write to *Penguin Books S. A., C. San Bernardo 117–6° E–28015 Madrid*

In Italy: Please write to *Penguin Italia s.r.l., Via Felice Casati 20, I–20124 Milano*

In France: Please write to *Penguin France S. A., 17 rue Lejeune, F–31000 Toulouse*

In Japan: Please write to *Penguin Books Japan, Ishikiribashi Building, 2–5–4, Suido, Tokyo 112*

In Greece: Please write to *Penguin Hellas Ltd, Dimocritou 3, GR–106 71 Athens*

In South Africa: Please write to *Longman Penguin Southern Africa (Pty) Ltd, Private Bag X08, Bertsham 2013*

READ MORE IN PENGUIN

CRITICAL STUDIES

Described by *The Times Educational Supplement* as 'admirable' and 'superb', Penguin Critical Studies is a specially developed series of critical essays on the major works of literature for use by students in universities, colleges and schools.

Titles published or in preparation include:

William Blake
The Changeling
Doctor Faustus
Emma and Persuasion
Great Expectations
The Great Gatsby
Heart of Darkness
The Poetry of Gerard
  Manley Hopkins
Joseph Andrews
Mansfield Park
Middlemarch
The Mill on the Floss
Paradise Lost
The Poetry of Alexander
  Pope

The Portrait of a Lady
A Portrait of the Artist as a
  Young Man
The Return of the Native
Rosencrantz and Guildenstern
  are Dead
Sons and Lovers
Tennyson
Tess of the D'Urbervilles
To the Lighthouse
The Waste Land
Wordsworth
Wuthering Heights
Yeats

READ MORE IN PENGUIN

CRITICAL STUDIES

Described by *The Times Educational Supplement* as 'admirable' and 'superb', Penguin Critical Studies is a specially developed series of critical essays on the major works of literature for use by students in universities, colleges and schools.

Titles published or in preparation include:

SHAKESPEARE

Antony and Cleopatra
As You Like It
Hamlet
Julius Caesar
King Lear
A Midsummer Night's Dream
Much Ado About Nothing
Othello
Richard II
Romeo and Juliet
Shakespeare – Text into Performance
Shakespeare's History Plays
The Tempest
Troilus and Cressida
The Winter's Tale

CHAUCER

Chaucer
The Pardoner's Tale
The Prologue to the
  Canterbury Tales

READ MORE IN PENGUIN

POETRY LIBRARY

Arnold	Selected by Kenneth Allott
Blake	Selected by W. H. Stevenson
Browning	Selected by Daniel Karlin
Burns	Selected by Angus Calder and William Donnelly
Byron	Selected by A. S. B. Glover
Clare	Selected by Geoffrey Summerfield
Coleridge	Selected by Richard Holmes
Donne	Selected by John Hayward
Dryden	Selected by Douglas Grant
Hardy	Selected by David Wright
Herbert	Selected by W. H. Auden
Jonson	Selected by George Parfitt
Keats	Selected by John Barnard
Kipling	Selected by James Cochrane
Lawrence	Selected by Keith Sagar
Milton	Selected by Laurence D. Lerner
Pope	Selected by Douglas Grant
Rubáiyát of Omar Khayyám	Translated by Edward FitzGerald
Shelley	Selected by Isabel Quigley
Tennyson	Selected by W. E. Williams
Wordsworth	Selected by Nicholas Roe
Yeats	Selected by Timothy Webb

READ MORE IN PENGUIN

A SELECTION OF POETRY

American Verse
British Poetry Since 1945
Caribbean Verse in English
Contemporary American Poetry
Contemporary British Poetry
English Poetry 1918–60
English Romantic Verse
English Verse
First World War Poetry
German Verse
Greek Verse
Irish Verse
Japanese Verse
Love Poetry
The Metaphysical Poets
Modern African Poetry
New Poetry
Poetry of the Thirties
Scottish Verse
Spanish Verse
Women Poets

READ MORE IN PENGUIN

INTERNATIONAL POETS – A SELECTION

Octavio Paz Selected Poems
Winner of the 1990 Nobel Prize for Literature

'His poetry allows us to glimpse a different and future place ... liberating and affirming' – James Wood in the *Guardian*

Fernando Pessoa Selected Poems

'I have sought for his shade in those Edwardian cafés in Lisbon which he haunted, for he was Lisbon's Cavafy or Verlaine' – Cyril Connolly in the *Sunday Times*

Yehuda Amichai Selected Poems
Translated by Chana Bloch and Stephen Mitchell

'A truly major poet ... there's a depth, breadth and weighty momentum in these subtle and delicate poems of his' – Ted Hughes

Czesław Miłosz Collected Poems 1931–1987
Winner of the 1980 Nobel Prize for Literature

'One of the greatest poets of our time, perhaps the greatest' – Joseph Brodsky

Joseph Brodsky To Urania
Winner of the 1987 Nobel Prize for Literature

Exiled from the Soviet Union in 1972, Joseph Brodsky has been universally acclaimed as the most talented Russian poet of his generation.

and

Paul Celan	Selected Poems
Tony Harrison	Selected Poems *and* Theatre Works 1973–1985
Heine	Selected Verse
Geoffrey Hill	Collected Poems
Philippe Jaccottet	Selected Poems
Osip Mandelstam	Selected Poems
Peter Redgrove	Poems 1954–1987